MONTEGO BAY TRAVE

From Reggae Beats to Tropical Retreats:
Unleashing the Magic of Jamaica with 7 Days
Itinerary Perfect for First-Timers

Patsy J. Tour

Copyright©2023Patsy J. Tour

All Rights Reserved

MONTEGI BAY TRAVEL GUIDE 2023

Patsy J. Tour

MONTEGO BAY
Travel Guide
2023

From Reggae Beats to Tropical Retreats: Unleashing the Magic of Jamaica with 7 Days Itinerary Perfect for First-Timers.

TABLE OF CONTENTS

INTRODUCTION — 10

CHAPTER 1 — 14

WELCOME TO MONTEGO BAY — 14
CLIMATE AND GEOGRAPHY — 14
BACKGROUND AND HISTORY — 15
POLITICAL CULTURE — 16
TOURISM AND THE ECONOMY — 17
INTERESTING REASONS WHY YOU SHOULD VISIT MONTEGO BAY — 19
15 THINGS SHOULD YOU KNOW BEFORE VISITING MONTEGO BAY — 22
THE DOS AND DON'TS FOR ALL TOURISTS TO MONTEGO BAY? — 27

CHAPTER 2 — 33

PLANNING YOUR TRIP TO MONTEGO BAY — 33
HOW TO PLAN A TRIP TO MONTEGO BAY — 33
MONTEGO BAY VISA REQUIREMENTS — 38
STEP-BY-STEP INSTRUCTIONS FOR ACQUIRING A VISA TO MONTEGO BAY — 40
THE BEST TIME TO VISIT MONTEGO BAY — 43
GETTING TO MONTEGO BAY — 48
MAJOR AIRLINES FROM EUROPE TO MONTEGO BAY — 51
TRANSPORTATION IN AND AROUND MONTEGO BAY — 53

CHAPTER 3 — 56

ACCOMMODATION OPTION IN MONTEGO BAY	56
HOTEL AND RESORT	59
VACATION RENTALS FOR USERS	62
ALL-INCLUSIVE RESORTS	65
BUDGET-FRIENDLY, MID-RANGE, AND LUXURY HOSTELS.	68
3-DAY ITINERARY IN MONTEGO BAY.	71
7-DAY ITINERARY IN MONTEGO BAY	73

CHAPTER 4 — 79

SAFETY AND TRAVEL TIPS	79
PRECAUTIONS FOR HEALTH AND SAFETY	79
ETIQUETTE AND LOCAL CUSTOMS	82
CURRENCY AND MONEY ISSUES	86
EMERGENCY CONTACTS FOR USERS	89

CHAPTER 5 — 92

LOCAL CUISINE AND DINNING	92
OVERVIEW OF JAMAICAN CUISINE	92
MUST-TRY RECIPES	96
MONTEGO BAY'S MOST POPULAR RESTAURANTS	99

CHAPTER 6 — 103

EXPLORING MONTEGO BAY	103
HIP STRIP IN MONTEGO BAY	103
PURCHASING	107

BARS AND RESTAURANTS	110
ENTERTAINMENT AT NIGHT	114
DOCTOR'S CAVE BEACH	118
ROSE HALL GREAT HOUSE	122
CROYDON PLANTATION	126
RAFTING ON THE MARTHA BRAE RIVER	130
MONTEGO BAY MARINE PARK	134
MONTEGO BAY CULTURAL CENTRE	138

CHAPTER 7 — 142

WHAT TO DO IN MANTEGO BAY (OUTDOOR ACTIVITIES)	142
PARK AND DUNN'S RIVER FALLS	142
CHUKKA CARIBBEAN ADVENTURES	146
RIDING A HORSE	150
CANOPY AND ZIPLINE TOURS	154
SNORKELING AND SCUBA DIVING	158
CATAMARAN CRUISES	162
MONTEGO BAY GOLFING	167

CHAPTER 8 — 171

EVENTS AND FESTIVALS IN MONTEGO BAY	171
REGGAE SUMFEST	171
JAMAICA FOOD & DRINK FESTIVAL	174
CELEBRATION OF BOB MARLEY'S BIRTHDAY	178

CHAPTER 9 — 183

USEFUL PHRASES AND VOCABULARY	183
COMMON JAMAICAN EXPRESSIONS	183
BASIC JAMAICAN PATOIS PHRASES	187

CHAPTER 10 — 191

DAY TRIP & NEARBY DESTINATION	191
NEGRIL	191
OCHO RIOS	194
FALMOUTH	198
KINGSTON	202

CHAPTER 11 — 206

SHOPPING IN MONTEGO BAY	206
CRAFT FAIRS	206
DUTY-FREE SHOPPING	210
SOUVENIRS AND LOCAL PRODUCTS	215

CONCLUSION — 220

INTRODUCTION

As I got off the airport and entered the bustling city of Montego Bay, it was a lovely morning. Excitement raced through me as I realized the following several days will be filled with wonderful activities and treasured memories. I had no idea that an unexpected meeting would turn my journey into something absolutely amazing. I walked out towards the famed Montego Bay Hip Strip, eager to investigate. As I wandered along, appreciating the colorful stores and listening to the melodious sounds of reggae music, the bustling mood surrounded me. The aroma of jerk chicken floated through the air with each step, tantalizing my taste senses and enticing me to a real Jamaican gastronomic experience.

The rhythmic sounds of a live band drew my attention as I entered a tiny, lively eatery. I took a seat near the stage, eager to immerse myself in the local culture. The upbeat tunes connected with the audience, infusing the air with excitement and celebration. As I tasted the savory spices of my jerk chicken, I couldn't help but tap my feet to the irresistible beat. I started into a discussion with the couple seated next to me, who were mesmerized by the music. Marcus and Simone described themselves as two residents who were genuinely enthusiastic about their nation and wanted to convey its charms. Their genuine friendliness and warmth immediately made me feel like a member of their extended family. Marcus recommended we go to Doctor's Cave Beach, a fabled location known for its crystal-clear turquoise seas and immaculate white beach. I happily consented, and soon we were walking along the beach, waves softly licking our feet. We swam, splashed, and laughed our way across the Caribbean water, forging an unbreakable relationship.

Marcus and Simone invited me to visit the majestic Rose Hall Great House the next day. As we went around the vast house, I couldn't help but be enthralled by stories of Annie Palmer, the infamous "White Witch" who once ruled the plantation. Marcus told the stories with such passion that, despite the warm Jamaican sun, I felt myself shivering.

We went to Croydon Plantation, a verdant sanctuary situated in the green hillsides, to get away from the history-laden atmosphere. As we wandered through the orchards, eating luscious pineapples and relishing the delicious nectar of mangoes, the lovely perfume of tropical fruits pervaded the air. It was a sensory experience that made an unforgettable impression on my taste receptors. Marcus surprised us with a journey down the Martha Brae River on our last day together. We boarded a peaceful bamboo raft, escorted by an experienced raft captain who regaled us with anecdotes about the river's history and the rich animals that made it home. As we sailed over the calm waters, shrouded by a lush canopy, a sensation of peace flooded over me, and I knew that this moment would live on in my heart forever. As I said goodbye to Marcus and Simone with a grateful heart, I realized that it was the unexpected connections and accidental meetings that made my trip to Montego Bay so remarkable. Beyond the breathtaking scenery and lively culture, it was the people that brought every moment to life, converting a holiday into an amazing spiritual trip.

I departed Montego Bay with a renewed sense of adventure and an insatiable appetite for travel, knowing that the experiences I had made will always have a special place in my heart. As I boarded the aircraft, a sensation of wanderlust awoke within me, desiring to explore new places, make new connections, and embark on many more spectacular experiences that were ahead.

Montego Bay is now a booming tourist destination, drawing people from all over the globe with its stunning beaches, lively culture, and numerous activities.

Political Culture

Like the rest of Jamaica, Montego Bay is governed by a parliamentary democracy. The nation acquired independence from British colonial authority in 1962 and is currently a constitutional monarchy, with the British monarch represented as the head of state by a governor-general. Multiple political parties affect the political scene of Montego Bay, with the two largest ones being the Jamaica Labour Party (JLP) and the People's National Party (PNP). Elections are conducted on a regular basis, and Montego Bay residents actively engage in the political process.

Montego Bay has a diverse cultural legacy that is inspired by its Afro-Caribbean origins. The city is well-known for its music, notably reggae, a Jamaican genre. At local taverns, clubs, and music festivals, visitors may enjoy the energetic beats, catchy rhythms, and beautiful melodies.

Montego Bay residents are recognized for their friendliness, kindness, and love of festivities. Festivals and events such as Reggae Sumfest and the Jamaica Food and Drink Festival highlight the region's rich cultural traditions, gastronomic delicacies, and creative abilities.

Tourism and the Economy

Tourism is a significant economic engine in Montego Bay. Every year, millions of visitors flock to the city's stunning beaches, opulent resorts, and diverse choice of activities. The tourist sector creates jobs, supports local companies, and adds to the region's general economic prosperity. Montego Bay also functions as a commercial hub with a lively downtown area and a free trade zone, drawing investors and cultivating trade partnerships with international partners.

Montego Bay, with its gorgeous beaches, tropical environment, rich history, and active cultural heritage, is a lively and intriguing destination. The natural beauty of the city, along with its friendly and inviting environment, make it a popular option for those looking for leisure, adventure, and an immersive Jamaican experience.

Interesting Reasons Why You Should Visit Montego Bay

Montego Bay, with its tempting combination of natural beauty, cultural depth, and friendly friendliness, provides several reasons to come. Montego Bay offers something for everyone, whether you want to relax on gorgeous beaches, participate in exciting adventure activities, or immerse yourself in colorful Jamaican culture. Let's look at the compelling reasons why a trip to Montego Bay should be on your schedule.

Beautiful Beaches: Montego Bay has some of the most beautiful beaches in the Caribbean. The coastline provides smooth beaches, crystal-clear blue seas, and tranquil environs, from the world-famous Doctor's Cave Beach to the hidden beauty of Dead End Beach. Whether you like sunbathing, swimming, snorkeling, or just relaxing with a tropical drink in hand, Montego Bay's beaches are the ideal place to rest and rejuvenate.

Immerse yourself in the colorful Jamaican culture that pervades Montego Bay via music and culture. With its throbbing rhythms and deep songs, the city is a reggae music hotspot. Participate in vibrant dancehall sessions, go to local pubs and clubs to see live performances, or go to music festivals like Reggae Sumfest to feel the addictive beat that fills the air. Montego Bay's cultural legacy is also celebrated via art, artisan fairs, and traditional gastronomic delights.

Excursions & Adventure: Montego Bay has a variety of exciting activities for adventure seekers. Zip over the thick rainforest canopy, enjoy horseback riding along the beach, or go river rafting down the Martha Brae River. Scuba diving and snorkeling are great ways to experience undersea delights, or take a catamaran tour to discover secret coves and beautiful reefs. Montego Bay offers many chances for exploration and adventure, from adrenaline-pumping excursions to peaceful nature encounters.

Historical sites: Learn about Montego Bay's history by visiting its unique sites. With its stately Georgian architecture and unsettling narratives, the Rose Hall Great House gives a window into the past. Discover the old St. James Parish Church and Sam Sharpe Square, named for a national hero who battled for liberation. These locations help visitors have a better knowledge of the region's rich history as well as its people's hardships and successes.

Culinary Delights: Jamaican cuisine is known for its flavorful spices and unique combination of African, European, and Asian influences. excellent delicacies include jerk chicken, curry goat, ackee and saltfish, and excellent burgers. Montego Bay is densely packed with restaurants and small eateries where you may appreciate real Jamaican cuisine and sample the island's gastronomic treasures.

Warm Hospitality: The warm and inviting demeanor of the people of Montego Bay is one of the most compelling reasons to come. Jamaicans are well-known for their warm grins, lively personalities, and genuine hospitality. Engage in local interactions, immerse yourself in their culture, and allow their warmth and friendliness enrich your Montego Bay experience.

Montego Bay entices visitors with its beautiful beaches, lively culture, adventurous adventures, historical sites, delectable food, and kind hospitality. Whether you're looking for leisure, excitement, or cultural immersion, Montego Bay provides everything you need for an amazing trip. Embrace the appeal of this Jamaican treasure and make memories that last a lifetime.

15 Things should you know before visiting Montego Bay

Before traveling to Montego Bay, it's a good idea to be informed of some crucial details to guarantee a pleasant and pleasurable journey. Here are 15 things you should know before visiting Montego Bay, with explanations:

- Check the entrance requirements for Jamaica to verify you have the required visa or travel papers.

Most travelers from the United States, Canada, and the United Kingdom do not need a visa for short-term visits.

- The Jamaican dollar (JMD) is the country's official currency. It's a good idea to have some local money on hand for little purchases, although US dollars are generally accepted at most tourist attractions.
- Language: Because English is the official language of Jamaica, most tourists will have little trouble communicating. Locals also speak Jamaican Patois, a local dialect, which adds to the cultural experience.
- Measures: As with any trip location, it is important to follow basic safety measures. Keep an eye out for strangers, avoid lonely locations at night, and keep your possessions safe. It is advised to utilize trustworthy transportation providers and to get local advice about safe neighborhoods and places.
- Weather & Packing: Because Montego Bay has a tropical environment, bring lightweight,

breathable clothes that is appropriate for warm temps. Remember to bring sunscreen, hats, and bug repellent. For milder nights or air-conditioned settings, bring a light sweater or jacket.

- Montego Bay has a variety of transportation alternatives, including taxis, rental automobiles, and scheduled trips. Taxis with red license plates are official and should be utilized to guarantee safety and fair pricing. Before you enter, haggle over rates.
- Beaches in Montego Bay are open to the public, however certain parts may be tied to special resorts. While enjoying the beaches, please respect other people's privacy. Avoid leaving personal items unsecured and observe local norms and rules.
- Tipping: Tipping is expected in Jamaica. It is customary to tip hotel, restaurant, and tour guide workers. The industry typical is 10-15% of the bill or service fee.

- Electricity: The voltage in Montego Bay is 110-120V, which is the same as in North America. If your gadgets utilize a different voltage or have various plug types, bring an adaptor.
- Before flying to Montego Bay, consult your healthcare professional about any required vaccines or health precautions. It's also a good idea to drink bottled water and use care while eating street cuisine.
- Time Zone: Montego Bay observes Eastern Standard Time (EST) and does not observe Daylight Saving Time. Make appropriate travel arrangements.
- Local Customs and Respect: To demonstrate respect for the local culture, learn about Jamaican customs and traditions. To communicate with the locals, learn a few basic pleasantries and words. They respect people who make an effort to accept their culture.
- Wi-Fi and mobile connections are available at most hotels, resorts, and cafés. Depending on your mobile service provider, international

roaming may be possible. Another alternative for Internet and calls is to get a local SIM card.

- Excursions & Tours: Montego Bay has a number of thrilling excursions and tours available, including snorkeling, river rafting, and seeing historical places. To guarantee a flawless experience, research and schedule these activities ahead of time.
- Montego Bay has a variety of shopping options, including artisan markets and duty-free boutiques. Although bargaining is prevalent at artisan markets, most establishments have set pricing. When buying local souvenirs, be sure they are real and of high quality.

You'll be well-prepared for a delightful and memorable stay to Montego Bay if you keep these crucial considerations in mind.

The Dos and Don'ts for all tourists to Montego Bay?

Dos:

- Respect local customs and traditions: Jamaicans are proud of their culture; express your appreciation by learning about their rituals and traditions. Greet locals with a friendly smile, speak politely, and be willing to learn from their experiences.
- Wear modestly while visiting public areas: While Montego Bay has a laid-back vibe, it's polite to wear modestly when visiting public locations, particularly religious institutions. Outside of beach areas, avoid wearing exposing apparel or swimwear.

- Try traditional Jamaican cuisine: traditional Jamaican cuisine is a highlight of every trip to Montego Bay. Local specialties include jerk chicken, ackee and saltfish, and curry goat. Discover the tastes and spices that distinguish Jamaican food.
- Do bargain in craft markets: Bargaining is normal while shopping at artisan markets. Negotiate in a courteous manner while being respectful to the suppliers. It's a chance to obtain a good deal while also enjoying the interaction process.
- Do use sun protection: the tropical environment of Montego Bay implies powerful solar radiation. Sunburn may be avoided by using sunscreen, wearing a hat, and finding shade during peak hours of sunshine.
- Try the indigenous fruits and beverages: Jamaica is famous for its fresh and unusual fruits. Enjoy delectable goodies such as fresh coconut water, mangoes, pineapples, and soursop. Also, don't pass up the opportunity to sample native

beverages such as rum punch or a refreshing fruit smoothie.
- To guarantee safety, utilize licensed taxis or scheduled transportation services suggested by your hotel or tour organizer. Confirm the fee before beginning the trip, and avoid taking rides from strangers.

- Beyond the resort districts: While Montego Bay's resorts provide luxury and convenience, journey beyond the tourist zones to find the city's original charm. To obtain a real experience of Jamaican culture, interact with people, tour local markets, and visit historical places.
- While credit cards are generally accepted at big places, it is suggested to bring cash in small quantities for local vendors, taxis, and smaller stores. This provides convenience and prevents any problems associated with change.
- Do engage in responsible tourism by keeping the environment and local people in mind. Respect the natural environment, properly dispose of

rubbish, and support local businesses and craftspeople. Consider taking part in sustainable tourism activities that encourage responsible tourism.

Don'ts:

- Respect local customs and traditions: Avoid making disparaging remarks or making jokes about Jamaican culture or religion. Local customs, such as religious ceremonies or social conventions, should be respected, even if they vary from your own.
- Excessive money or jewels should not be displayed: Avoid showing off valuable jewelry, devices, or huge sums of money in public. This decreases the possibility of becoming a victim of theft or unwanted attention.
- Drink bottled water or water from recognized sources instead of tap water to prevent any health problems. while in doubt, use bottled water while

brushing your teeth or order beverages without ice.
- Don't go out alone at night in unknown areas: It's advised to avoid wandering alone in unfamiliar or poorly lit locations, particularly at night, as with any trip. Avoid densely crowded and well-lit places, and instead arrange for transportation via reliable sources.
- Don't litter or hurt the environment: Help maintain Montego Bay's natural beauty by properly disposing of rubbish and avoiding behaviors that may affect the environment. Respect protected places and follow responsible eco-tourism norms.
- Don't participate in unlawful activities: It's essential to follow Jamaican laws and regulations. Avoid any criminal activity, such as drug usage, buying counterfeit items, or engaging in any type of exploitation.
- Don't bother the locals too much: While Jamaicans are polite and inviting, personal space and limits must be respected. Avoid being

obtrusive or photographing individuals without their permission.

- Avoid excessive public drinking: Excessive public drinking is often frowned upon in Jamaica. Consume alcoholic drinks sensibly and keep in mind local laws surrounding public drunkenness.
- Do not disregard water safety precautions: When engaging in water activities, obey all safety rules and recommendations. Take note of any cautions about currents, tides, or dangerous situations. When required, always use a life jacket.
- Don't forget to bring travel insurance: Travel insurance that covers medical emergencies, vacation cancellations, and lost things is always suggested. This gives you piece of mind and financial security when visiting Montego Bay.

You may have a courteous, fun, and safe experience while touring the colorful city of Montego Bay if you follow these dos and don'ts.

CHAPTER 2

Planning Your Trip to Montego Bay

How to Plan a Trip to Montego Bay

Planning a vacation to Montego Bay may be a thrilling experience. Here are some ideas to consider while organizing your vacation to guarantee a smooth and pleasurable experience:

Determine the Best Time to Visit: Montego Bay has mild weather all year, although the busiest tourist season is from December to April. Consider going during the shoulder season (May to June or September to November) to avoid crowds and maybe save money.

Make a Budget: Create a budget and allot monies for lodging, transportation, food, activities, and mementos. To help you manage your budget, look at the typical prices of lodging, restaurants, and activities in Montego Bay.

Choose your lodging: Montego Bay has a variety of lodging alternatives, including luxury resorts, boutique hotels, guesthouses, and vacation rentals. When choosing your lodging, consider variables such as location, facilities, and budget.

Investigate and Plan Activities: Investigate the sights and activities available in Montego Bay and plan an itinerary based on your preferences. Plan your activities ahead of time to make the most of your time, whether it's seeing historical places, enjoying water sports, or immersing yourself in local culture.

Check Travel Requirements: Ensure that you have all of the essential travel documentation to enter Jamaica. Check the validity of your passport and any visa requirements relevant to your nationality. To minimize surprises, familiarize yourself with entrance and customs laws.

Search for airline choices to Montego Bay and book your tickets well in advance to receive the best rates. Consider being flexible with your vacation dates or using flight comparison tools to locate the best deals.

Consider Travel Insurance: Travel insurance that covers medical emergencies, vacation cancellations, and lost possessions is recommended. Examine several insurance to discover one that meets your requirements and offers appropriate coverage for your vacation.

Jamaican phrases and pleasantries: While English is commonly spoken, learning a few basic Jamaican phrases and pleasantries will improve your relationships with locals and demonstrate your admiration for their culture. "Hello," "thank you," and "excuse me" may all go a long way.

Check the weather forecast for Montego Bay for your vacation dates and prepare suitable attire. Sunscreen, hats, bug repellant, swimsuits, and comfortable walking shoes are all must-haves. Remember to bring any required prescriptions or travel adapters.

Research Local Customs and Etiquette: To show respect to the people, familiarize yourself with Jamaican customs and etiquette. Because Jamaicans place a high importance on politeness and friendliness, respecting cultural standards may improve your relationships and experiences.

Check Health and Safety Recommendations: Speak with your healthcare physician or contact a travel clinic to learn about any Jamaican immunizations or health precautions. To protect your safety, follow fundamental safety principles, be aware of your surroundings, and take the appropriate steps.

Keep up to date on COVID-19 travel standards and limitations for Jamaica, including any testing or vaccine requirements, quarantine regulations, and local health and safety precautions. Keep up to current on travel warnings issued by your home country and the Jamaican authorities.

While US dollars are frequently accepted, consider converting some for Jamaican dollars for smaller purchases, local markets, and transportation. Learn about currency rates and use caution while using ATMs or exchanging money.

Investigate Transportation Options: Investigate the various modes of transportation accessible in Montego Bay, such as taxis, vehicle rentals, and public transit. Based on your scheduled activities and preferences, choose the most convenient and cost-effective solutions.

Connect with Local Resources: To learn more about Montego Bay, join online travel groups, read travel blogs, or speak with locals. Their own knowledge may give vital information and assist you in making educated judgments.

By following these suggestions, you may plan a well-organized and unforgettable vacation to Montego Bay, assuring a terrific time in this lovely area.

Montego Bay Visa Requirements

Visa requirements for Montego Bay, Jamaica vary by country. The following are some basic recommendations for visa requirements:

Visa-Free Entry: Certain nations' citizens do not need a visa to enter Jamaica for tourist reasons. The United nations, Canada, the United Kingdom, European Union member nations, Australia, and New Zealand are classic examples. The period of a visa-free stay might range from 30 to 90 days.

Visa on Arrival: Certain nations qualify for a visa on arrival. This means you may get a visa in Montego Bay without needing to apply ahead of time. Visitors from Brazil, Colombia, Mexico, and South Korea may take use of this option. The length of stay given upon arrival may vary.

Visitors from countries that are not eligible for visa-free entry or visa on arrival must get a visa before going to Montego Bay from a Jamaican embassy or consulate in their home country. Typically, the visa application procedure includes completing an application form, supporting papers, and paying the required costs.

By calling the closest Jamaican embassy or consulate or visiting their official website, you should be able to determine the precise visa requirements for your nationality and intended period of stay. They will provide you the most up-to-date and correct information on visa requirements and application processes.

Furthermore, during the COVID-19 pandemic, visitors visiting Jamaica should be aware of any unique entry criteria, testing or vaccine requirements, or quarantine processes that may be in place. For the most up-to-date information and travel warnings, see the Jamaican government's official website or call the closest Jamaican embassy or consulate.

Step-by-step instructions for acquiring a visa to Montego Bay

Obtaining a visa to visit Montego Bay, Jamaica may differ based on your nationality and the particular criteria of the Jamaican embassy or consulate in your country. However, here is a general step-by-step procedure to help you with your visa application:

Determine the kind of visa required: Go to the website of the Jamaican embassy or consulate in your country to find out what kind of visa you need. This might include a tourist visa, a business visa, or another category depends on the reason for your stay.

Gather necessary papers: Go through the list of documents needed for the visa application. A completed visa application form, a valid passport with at least six months validity, recent passport-sized photographs, proof of travel itinerary (such as flight bookings), proof of Montego Bay accommodation, financial statements or bank statements demonstrating sufficient funds for your stay, and a letter of invitation (if applicable) are all common documents.

Complete the visa application form: Download the visa application form from the website of the Jamaican embassy or consulate, or request it in person. Fill out the form fully and properly, including all needed information.

Prepare supporting documentation: Make photocopies of any necessary supporting documentation. Ensure that all papers are current, legitimate, and satisfy the precise standards given by the Jamaican embassy or consulate.

Pay the visa fee: Confirm the visa fee amount and authorized payment methods. Pay the visa fee as directed by the embassy or consulate. As evidence of payment, save the payment receipt.

Submit the application: To submit your visa application, go to the Jamaican embassy or consulate in your country within their official business hours. Bring the completed application form, supporting papers, and the receipt for the visa fee payment. Some embassies or consulates may need you to make an appointment ahead of time.

Attend an interview (if necessary): You may be needed to attend an interview at the embassy or consulate, depending on your nationality or the particular circumstances of your application. Prepare for the interview by checking your trip arrangements, answering questions about your visit's purpose, and giving any extra information asked.

Follow the progress of your application: After you submit your application, the embassy or consulate will give you with a tracking number or receipt. This may be used to follow the progress of your application using their online system or by calling the embassy or consulate directly.

Collect the visa: The embassy or consulate will notify you after your visa application has been granted. To get your visa, go to the embassy or consulate during the scheduled collecting hours. Bring your original passport as well as any other documentation necessary by the embassy or consulate.

It's crucial to remember that this is just a broad overview of the visa application process; exact criteria and processes may vary depending on your nationality and the Jamaican embassy or consulate in your country. For the most current and up-to-date information on visa application requirements and processes, check the official website of the Jamaican embassy or consulate or contact them directly.

The Best time to visit Montego Bay

The ideal time to visit Montego Bay, Jamaica is determined by your tastes and the activities you want to do during your vacation. Montego Bay has a tropical environment with pleasant temperatures all year, making it an appealing resort all year. However, there are several considerations to consider while deciding when to come. Here's a detailed breakdown of the best times to visit Montego Bay:

Maximum Season (December through April):

The busiest tourist season in Montego Bay is during the winter months, when many visitors flee colder locations to enjoy the pleasant Caribbean weather. This time of year is distinguished by dry and sunny weather, making it ideal for beach activities, water sports, and outdoor exploration. However, expect greater crowds and increased lodging expenses around this period. If you want to travel during the high season, it is best to reserve your lodgings well in advance.

Shoulder Season (May through June and September through November):

When compared to the peak season, the shoulder seasons provide a more balanced combination of excellent weather and less visitors. May to June and September to November are considered transitional months, with somewhat decreased rainfall and nevertheless warm and pleasant temperatures. If you prefer a calmer environment and want to take advantage of possibly reduced pricing on lodgings and activities, the shoulder season is a terrific time to come.

Season of Hurricanes (June to November):

Montego Bay is located inside the hurricane belt, and the Caribbean's official hurricane season spans from June to November. While the likelihood of experiencing a hurricane is minimal, it is important to be informed of weather conditions and monitor any possible tropical storms or hurricanes before arranging your trip. During this time, travel insurance that covers trip cancellations due to extreme weather is suggested.

Summer (July through August):

The months of July and August are considered low season in Montego Bay. These months coincide with many families' summer vacations, resulting in a minor increase in visits. However, it is still less congested than during the high season. Accommodation and airfare prices may be more reasonable at this season, making it an appealing choice for budget-conscious tourists.

Festivals and Special Events:

Throughout the year, Montego Bay organizes a variety of festivals and events that provide distinct cultural experiences. The Reggae Sumfest, held in July, is a prominent event that highlights Jamaica's robust reggae music sector. In January, the Air Jamaica Jazz and Blues Festival attracts music fans from all around the globe. Searching the event calendar might help you schedule your trip around certain festivals or events that interest you.

Rainfall Consideration:

Montego Bay has a tropical climate, and rain may fall at any time of year. The wettest months, however, are typically between May and October, with June, September, and October getting the most precipitation.

You may still enjoy your stay to Montego Bay if you don't mind the odd rain and want to take advantage of possible cost reductions during the low season.

To summarize, the ideal time to visit Montego Bay depends on your weather, crowd, and financial choices. Peak season delivers dry and bright weather but also greater crowds and higher pricing. The shoulder season offers an excellent mix of nice weather and less visitors. The low season may offer lower pricing, but it also corresponds with hurricane season. Consider your objectives, money, and hobbies to choose the optimum time for you.

Getting to Montego Bay

Montego Bay, Jamaica is a popular tourist location with well-connected transportation options, so getting there is quite simple. The following are the most typical methods to get to Montego Bay:

By Air:

Sangster International Airport (MBJ), Jamaica's busiest airport, serves Montego Bay. It gets a large number of foreign flights from important cities all around the globe. Direct flights to Montego Bay are available from a variety of locations, including North America, Europe, and the Caribbean. The airport is within a short distance from the city center upon arrival, making it handy for passengers.

By Cruise Line:

If you're thinking of taking a cruise, Montego Bay is a popular port of call for many cruise companies. Many Caribbean cruises feature a port of call in Montego Bay, where guests may disembark and explore the city and its surrounding attractions. The Montego Bay Cruise Port provides amenities and services for cruise ship guests.

By Car:

If you're already in Jamaica or a neighboring city, you may drive to Montego Bay. The North Coast Highway (A1) links Montego Bay to other significant towns and communities on Jamaica's northern coast. This picturesque route provides stunning views of the coastline and is a popular alternative for people who like a road trip.

By Bus:

Between Montego Bay and other towns and cities in Jamaica, public buses, often known as "route taxis" or "coasters," run. However, keep in mind that some buses may be overcrowded and have restricted itineraries. Private bus services and tour companies, on the other hand, provide transportation choices for travelers, including shuttle services between Montego Bay and renowned tourist locations.

Traveling by Private Vehicle:

Hiring a cab or renting a vehicle are two private transportation choices. Taxis are readily accessible at the airport, hotels, and popular tourist destinations. It's best to use registered taxis or organize transportation via trusted companies. Renting a vehicle allows you to explore Montego Bay and its surroundings at your own time. There are many automobile rental firms near the airport and across the city.

Consider your location, budget, and interests while planning your trip to Montego Bay to choose the best form of transportation. For foreign travelers, air travel is the most prevalent and convenient choice, while other forms of transportation give options for those already in Jamaica or the Caribbean area.

Major Airlines from Europe to Montego Bay

British Airways is a British airline.

The airline Air France

Lufthansa

Virgin Atlantic is a British airline.

TUI Airlines

Condor

Jet2

Royal Dutch Airlines (KLM)

Canada Air

American Airlines Inc.

These airlines often fly from major European cities including London, Paris, Amsterdam, Frankfurt, and

Munich to Montego Bay. Flight itineraries and pricing may vary based on the precise departure location, time of year, and any existing discounts or offers.

I suggest utilizing major travel services like as Expedia, Skyscanner, Kayak, or directly visiting the websites of the airlines listed above to get the most accurate and up-to-date flight pricing. You may use these sites to search for flights based on your selected dates, compare costs, and purchase tickets. Signing up for airline newsletters or setting ticket alerts will also keep you up to date on any discounts or special deals.

When selecting an airline, keep in mind aspects like as luggage limitations, layover lengths, and overall travel experience. It's also a good idea to book your flights ahead of time to get the greatest discounts and availability.

Transportation in and Around Montego Bay

Getting about Montego Bay, Jamaica is quite simple, since guests have various transportation alternatives. The following are the most prevalent types of transportation in Montego Bay:

Taxis: Taxis are a popular and convenient mode of transportation in Montego Bay. Taxis are easily accessible at the airport, hotels, and tourist locations. It is advised to use legal taxis, which are distinguished by their red license plates. Negotiate the fee before beginning the trip, or utilize the meter. Taxis may also be rented for extended periods of time or for day excursions.

Route Taxis: Route taxis, commonly known as "coasters," are shared taxis that travel along designated routes throughout Montego Bay and the surrounding regions. They are often minivans or bigger vehicles with a route indication on the windshield. Route taxis have fixed prices and are a more cost-effective choice for short-distance travel inside the city. They may, however, be overcrowded and make many stops to pick up and drop off people.

Rental Cars: Renting a vehicle allows you to explore Montego Bay and its surroundings at your own leisure. Several automobile rental firms, including foreign brands, are available in the city. It is essential to obtain a valid driver's license and to get acquainted with Jamaican traffic laws and driving conditions. The roads in Montego Bay are well-kept, but be aware of local driving practices and road conditions.

Bicycle rentals are available in Montego Bay, enabling tourists to explore the city on two wheels. Bicycles may be leased for a few hours or for the whole day, making them an eco-friendly and leisurely mode of transportation. Some hotels and tour companies provide bicycle rentals, and the city also has specialized bicycle rental businesses.

Hotel Shuttles: Many Montego Bay hotels and resorts provide shuttle services to their visitors. Visitors may use these shuttles to major destinations, retail malls, and neighboring beaches. If you're staying at a hotel, enquire about shuttle service availability and scheduling.

Walking: The main core of Montego Bay is tiny and pedestrian-friendly. Walking may be a nice and quick method to get about if you're staying in the core region or visiting certain sites nearby. However, be careful while walking on crowded streets and keep an eye on your surroundings.

It is important to plan your routes, consider travel times, and be careful of your personal safety while utilizing any method of transportation in Montego Bay. Carry little cash or change for taxis, confirm rates in advance, and select reputable transportation providers. Consider traffic conditions as well, particularly during peak hours or significant events, since these might alter travel times.

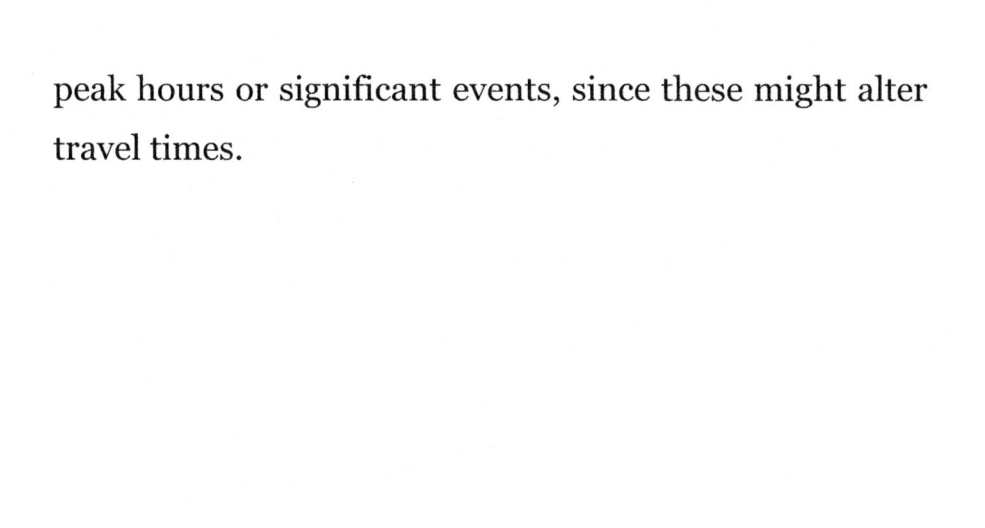

CHAPTER 3

Accommodation Option in Montego Bay

Alternatives for Accommodation

Montego Bay, Jamaica has a variety of lodging alternatives to meet a variety of budgets and interests. There are lots of options available for luxury resorts, all-inclusive hotels, charming guesthouses, and budget-friendly lodgings. Here are some popular Montego Bay lodging options:

Luxury Resorts: Montego Bay is well-known for its beautiful beachside resorts, which provide a variety of facilities and services. Private beaches, several pools, spa facilities, fine dining restaurants, and recreational activities are common features of these resorts. Sandals Montego Bay, Half Moon, Round Hill Hotel and Villas, and Hyatt Ziva Rose Hall are among well-known luxury resorts in Montego Bay.

All-Inclusive Hotels: Many Montego Bay hotels provide all-inclusive packages that include lodging, food, beverages, and access to numerous activities and facilities. These solutions are ideal for tourists who desire a stress-free trip. The Hilton Rose Hall Resort & Spa, Iberostar Grand Rose Hall, and Secrets Wild Orchid Montego Bay are among the most popular all-inclusive hotels in Montego Bay.

Montego Bay also has delightful boutique hotels that provide a more intimate and customized experience. These smaller motels often feature distinctive design, customized service, and a welcoming atmosphere. The Tryall Club, The Cliff Hotel, and The Caves are some of the boutique hotels in Montego Bay.

Guesthouses and Bed & Breakfasts: For a more affordable choice or a more authentic local experience, try staying at a guesthouse or bed and breakfast facility. These lodgings often provide comfortable rooms, pleasant hosts, and a more intimate setting. They may be found in both the city core and more remote places. Polkerris Bed & Breakfast and Toby's Resort are two examples.

Vacation rentals are another popular kind of lodging in Montego Bay. These may include short-term rentals of private villas, flats, or condominiums. Vacation rentals are ideal for families or parties seeking extra room, solitude, and the ability to prepare their own meals. Vacation rental websites such as Airbnb and HomeAway provide a choice of vacation rental possibilities in Montego Bay.

Consider aspects like as location, closeness to activities or the beach, facilities provided, pricing, and prior guest reviews when selecting your Montego Bay hotel. To ensure the greatest availability and costs, book your lodgings in advance, particularly during high travel seasons.

Hotel and Resort

ChatGPT Montego Bay, Jamaica is well-known for its diverse selection of hotels and resorts that accommodate to a variety of budgets, interests, and vacation types. From magnificent beachfront resorts to comfortable mid-range hotels, here are some significant Montego Bay hotel and resort options:

Half Moon: With its magnificent beachfront setting, large suites, and a variety of activities, this famous and award-winning resort provides a spectacular experience. Half Moon is home to a championship golf course, a world-class spa, many restaurants, pools, and a private Dolphin Lagoon.

Sandals Montego Bay: Sandals is a well-known all-inclusive resort brand, and its Montego Bay site offers an adults-only getaway in a beautiful beachfront setting. Gourmet cuisine, water sports, entertainment, and access to adjacent golf courses are available to guests.

Secrets St. James Montego Bay: This adults-only, all-inclusive resort is part of the Secrets Resorts & Spas brand and provides an intimate and refined setting. Elegant rooms, exquisite dining choices, a full-service spa, and access to a private beach are available to guests.

Iberostar Grand Rose Hall: This all-inclusive, adults-only resort features magnificent accommodations, various pools, exquisite dining choices, a spa, and a championship golf course on a stunning length of white sand beach. The resort offers a unique combination of luxury, leisure, and entertainment.

Hilton Rose Hall Resort & Spa: This family-friendly resort is located on the historic Rose Hall Plantation and provides a wide choice of facilities and activities. A water park, various pools, a private beach, golf, tennis, and a full-service spa are available to guests.

Hyatt Ziva Rose Hall: This all-inclusive, family-friendly resort has a fantastic beachfront setting as well as pools, a water park, a kids' club, and a spa. The resort caters to people of all ages, making it ideal for families.

Royalton Blue Waters: Royalton Blue Waters is a contemporary and fashionable all-inclusive resort with premium rooms, gourmet dining choices, numerous pools, a private beach, a spa, and a range of activities and entertainment for both adults and children.

Round Hill Hotel and Villas: This premium resort, located just outside of Montego Bay, combines traditional elegance with Jamaican charm. Round Hill is noted for its exceptional service and peacefulness, with tastefully decorated suites, private villas, a beach, spa, and several dining choices.

S Hotel Jamaica: This boutique hotel offers a trendy and contemporary ambience by integrating modern design with Jamaican cultural features. The hotel has elegant rooms, a rooftop pool and bar, a beach club, and a spa. In Montego Bay, it provides a dynamic and fashionable choice.

Deja Resort: Located in the middle of Montego Bay's Hip Strip, Deja Resort provides luxurious rooms as well as a convenient position among shopping, restaurants, and entertainment. There is a pool, a restaurant, and a rooftop lounge with panoramic views at the resort.

Consider your budget, preferred facilities, proximity to activities, and whether you want an all-inclusive or more autonomous experience when selecting a hotel or resort in Montego Bay. To ensure your desired lodging, it's best to read reviews, compare costs, and book ahead of time, particularly during high travel seasons.

Vacation Rentals for Users

Vacation rentals, in addition to hotels and resorts, are a popular lodging choice in Montego Bay, providing guests with a more autonomous and home-like experience. Here are some Montego Bay vacation rental options:

Private Villas: Montego Bay has several private villas available for short-term rental. These villas often have many bedrooms, private pools, beautiful gardens, and breathtaking ocean views. They provide a magnificent and isolated getaway that is ideal for families, parties, or couples looking for peace and space.

Condos and Apartments: There are several condos and apartments for rent in Montego Bay. These may vary from small studios to huge multi-bedroom condos in gated neighborhoods or on the beach. For individuals searching for self-catering lodgings, condos and flats are a pleasant and reasonable alternative.

Beachfront Cottages: Beachfront cottages may be a wonderful option for a more personal and rustic experience. These cottages are usually along the water's edge and provide direct access to the beach. They often have pleasant interiors, outdoor areas, and breathtaking views of the Caribbean Sea.

Guesthouses and Bed & Breakfasts: Some Montego Bay establishments provide guesthouse or bed and breakfast accommodations. These smaller facilities provide a more customized and homey experience, generally with comfortable rooms, social spaces, and breakfast. They may be an excellent alternative for budget-conscious tourists or those looking for a more local and intimate setting.

When looking for vacation rentals in Montego Bay, it's critical to do your homework and confirm the property's validity and dependability. It is best to book via reliable companies or platforms that provide reviews and safe payment choices. It's also a good idea to speak with the property owner or management directly to clarify any queries or specific requests.

Vacation rentals provide additional room, privacy, and the freedom to make your own meals or live like a local. They are ideal for extended visits, families, or groups of friends vacationing together. Furthermore, they often provide a one-of-a-kind and real Montego Bay experience.

All-Inclusive Resorts

All-inclusive resorts in Montego Bay give customers a hassle-free holiday experience by combining lodgings, meals, beverages, and numerous facilities. These resorts strive to offer a pleasant and convenient atmosphere in which visitors can relax and enjoy their stay without having to worry about extra costs. Here are some of the most well-known all-inclusive resorts in Montego Bay:

Sandals Montego Bay: Sandals is a well-known all-inclusive resort chain, and its Montego Bay location is one of their flagship properties. Sandals Montego Bay is located on a lovely length of beach and provides exquisite rooms, various restaurants and bars, water sports, entertainment, and access to surrounding golf courses.

Secrets St. James Montego Bay: This adults-only, all-inclusive resort is part of the Secrets Resorts & Spas brand and offers a refined and private setting. Gourmet restaurants, premium drinks, a full-service spa, and access to a private beach are available to guests.

Iberostar Grand Rose Hall: This adults-only, all-inclusive resort on a beautiful beach provides an exquisite and upmarket experience. It has opulent accommodations, exquisite cuisine, various pools, a spa, and a championship golf course.

Hilton Rose Hall Resort & Spa: This all-inclusive resort for families is set on the historic Rose Hall Plantation. It has a water park, various pools, a private beach, golf, tennis, and a full-service spa, among other attractions and activities for people of all ages.

Hyatt Ziva Rose Hall: With its beachfront location and comprehensive facilities, this all-inclusive resort appeals to families and couples. Guests may take use of a range of eating choices, as well as various pools, a water park, a kids' club, and a spa. Guests of all ages may enjoy entertainment and activities.

Royalton Blue Waters: This upmarket all-inclusive resort has upscale rooms, gourmet cuisine, numerous pools, a private beach, a spa, and a variety of activities and entertainment for both adults and children.

All-inclusive resorts provide visitors the convenience of having everything they need on-site, such as meals, beverages, entertainment, and recreational activities. They are very popular for weddings, family holidays, and other events. It is critical to research each resort's precise features and facilities, since they may differ. Furthermore, certain resorts may have age limitations or cater to adults or families only.

Consider aspects like as location, the quality of eating choices, the breadth of activities and entertainment provided, and feedback from prior guests before choosing an all-inclusive resort. To get the greatest availability and costs for all-inclusive resorts in Montego Bay, it's essential to book ahead of time, particularly during high travel seasons.

Budget-Friendly, Mid-Range, and Luxury Hostels.

Budget-Friendly Hostels:

Reggae Hostel Montego Bay: This hostel, located in the center of Montego Bay, provides dormitory-style dormitories and private rooms at reasonable rates. Prices begin at $20 per night. The hostel has a shared kitchen, common spaces, and a relaxed environment. The beach, shopping, and restaurants are all within walking distance.

Zanzi Beach Resort: Located in Freeport, Zanzi Beach Resort has affordable private rooms with communal bathrooms. Prices begin at $30 per night. There is a bar, a restaurant, and a pleasant outdoor pool area at the resort. It's not far from local attractions and beaches.

Mid-Range Hotels:

Toby's Resort: Toby's Resort, located on the famed Hip Strip, has pleasant accommodations, an outdoor pool, and a restaurant. Prices begin around $90 per night. Popular sights, commercial centers, and entertainment choices are all within walking distance of the hotel.

Gloucestershire Hotel: Located on the "Hip Strip," the Gloucestershire Hotel offers reasonably priced accommodations in a handy location. Prices begin at $80 per night. The hotel has a pool and a restaurant, as well as convenient access to beaches and entertainment sites.

Luxury Hostel

Round Hill Hotel and Villas: Located on a secluded cove, this premium resort provides exquisite suites, villas, and private cottages. Prices begin at $500 per night. The resort offers a variety of eating choices, a spa, a private beach, and water sports. It is a short drive from Montego Bay.

Secrets Wild Orchid Montego Bay: This all-inclusive adults-only resort offers premium rooms, exquisite dining choices, and a variety of facilities. Prices begin at $400 per night. The resort has a spa, many pools, water sports, and entertainment opportunities. It is set on a secluded beach.

Please keep in mind that the rates shown are estimates and may change based on the season, accommodation type, and availability. For the most current and up-to-date price information, contact the lodgings directly or use reliable booking services.

3-Day Itinerary in Montego Bay.

Day 1:

Morning:

Arrive in Montego Bay and check into your accommodation.

Afternoon:
Explore the Hip Strip and visit local shops and boutiques for souvenir shopping.

Evening:
Enjoy dinner at a local restaurant, savoring Jamaican cuisine and soaking in the vibrant atmosphere.

Day 2:

Morning:
Visit Doctor's Cave Beach for a relaxing day by the crystal-clear waters and white sandy beaches.

Afternoon:

Take a boat tour to the Montego Bay Marine Park for snorkeling and exploring the colorful underwater world.

Evening:

Experience the lively nightlife in Montego Bay by visiting local bars and clubs for live music and dancing.

Day 3:

Morning:

Embark on an adventure to Dunn's River Falls in Ocho Rios. Climb the cascading waterfalls and take in the breathtaking views.

Afternoon:

Explore the historic Rose Hall Great House and learn about the legendary White Witch of Rose Hall.

Evening:

Enjoy a farewell dinner at a beachfront restaurant, savoring fresh seafood and watching the sunset over the Caribbean Sea.

7-Day Itinerary in Montego Bay

***Day 1-3:** Follow the 3-day itinerary mentioned above to explore Montego Bay's highlights, including the Hip Strip, Doctor's Cave Beach, Montego Bay Marine Park, Dunn's River Falls, and Rose Hall Great House.*

Day 4:

Morning:
Take a day trip to Negril and spend the day at Seven Mile Beach, known for its stunning white sand and turquoise waters.

Afternoon:
Visit Rick's Cafe and witness the famous cliff divers while enjoying the panoramic views.

Evening:

Return to Montego Bay and relax at your accommodation.

Day 5:

Morning:
Explore the vibrant city of Kingston, visiting the Bob Marley Museum, Devon House, and the National Gallery of Jamaica.

Afternoon:
Take a stroll through Emancipation Park and enjoy the peaceful atmosphere.

Evening:
Experience the local nightlife scene in Kingston, visiting live music venues and enjoying Jamaican rhythms.

Day 6:
Morning:
Discover the natural beauty of Falmouth by visiting Martha Brae River for a relaxing bamboo rafting experience.

Afternoon:

Explore the historic streets of Falmouth and visit the Georgian-style architecture and the Falmouth Craft Market.

Evening:

Return to Montego Bay and indulge in a fine dining experience at a luxury restaurant.

Day 7:

Morning:

Enjoy a day of adventure at Chukka Caribbean Adventures, participating in thrilling activities like ziplining, ATV tours, and horseback riding.

Afternoon:

Relax at a nearby beach or take a leisurely catamaran cruise along the coast.

Evening:

Bid farewell to Montego Bay with a sunset dinner cruise, enjoying the beautiful views and savoring delicious Caribbean cuisine.

These itineraries provide a mix of relaxation, adventure, cultural exploration, and natural beauty, allowing you to make the most of your time in Montego Bay and experience the diverse attractions that Jamaica has to offer.

CHAPTER 4

Safety and Travel Tips

Precautions for Health and Safety

When visiting Montego Bay, it is essential to prioritize your health and safety in order to have a pleasant and pleasurable trip. Here are some important health and safety considerations to remember:

Stay Hydrated: Because Jamaica's tropical environment may be hot and humid, it's crucial to drink lots of water throughout the day. Keep a water bottle on hand and replenish it as required.

Sun Protection: Because the sun in Montego Bay may be harsh, it is essential to protect yourself from sunburn and heatstroke. Wear high-SPF sunscreen, a hat, sunglasses, and lightweight, breathable clothes. During the warmest hours of the day, seek shade.

Use Mosquito Repellent: Mosquitoes may be found in several locations of Montego Bay, particularly around dark and morning. To avoid mosquito bites, use DEET-containing insect repellent to exposed skin and wear long-sleeved shirts and pants.

Swim Safely: While Montego Bay has lovely beaches and clean seas, it is crucial to swim safely. Swim only in authorized areas where lifeguards are present, and be aware of any posted warnings or flags indicating dangerous circumstances.

Consume Food and Water With prudence: To prevent foodborne infections, consume food and beverages with prudence. Consume bottled water instead of tap water, and make sure that any food you consume is properly cooked and prepared hygienically.

Use Safe transit: If you want to hire a vehicle or use public transit, be cautious on the roads. Follow traffic regulations in your area, use seat belts, and be mindful of your surroundings. For increased safety and convenience, consider choosing trusted taxi services or private transportation choices.

Take care to preserve your things: As with any tourist site, it is essential to take care to preserve your things. Keep your valuables in a hotel safe or lockbox, and avoid flaunting costly goods or huge sums of cash in public.

Respect Local Customs and Laws: To guarantee a courteous and trouble-free vacation, familiarize yourself with Jamaican customs and laws. When visiting holy locations, dress modestly, respect local customs, and avoid any unlawful activities or narcotics.

Stay Informed: Stay up to speed on the latest travel warnings and Montego Bay information. For any special rules or advice for travelers, contact your embassy or consulate.

Consider obtaining travel insurance that covers medical expenditures, trip cancellation, and other unexpected occurrences. This will provide you peace of mind and financial security in the event of an emergency or unforeseen occurrence.

By taking these health and safety measures, you will be able to enjoy your stay to Montego Bay with confidence, knowing that you have done the necessary efforts to safeguard yourself and have a safe and memorable trip.

Etiquette and Local Customs

When visiting Montego Bay, it's crucial to learn about the local traditions and etiquette in order to respect the culture and have great interactions with the people. Here are some important traditions and etiquette guidelines to remember:

Greetings: In general, Jamaicans are pleasant and hospitable. It is common to greet them with a cheerful "hello" or "good morning/afternoon/evening." Handshakes are also frequent when meeting someone for the first time.

Punctuality: When compared to other cultures, Jamaican time might be more loose. However, it is still necessary to be considerate of others' time. Arrive on time for planned appointments and meetings, but allow for a short delay in more casual circumstances.

Politeness and Respect: Jamaicans place a high priority on politeness and respect. while engaging with locals, use "please" and "thank you" whether at a restaurant, store, or while asking for directions. Being kind and respectful can help you make great relationships.

Dress Code: Although the attitude in Montego Bay is easygoing and informal, it is nevertheless vital to dress correctly, particularly when visiting religious sites or luxury places. While beachwear is fine, it is advised that you cover yourself while strolling around town or visiting other public locations.

Jamaicans often value personal space and may stand at a comfortable distance during chats. If you are not asked to enter someone's personal area, do not do so.

While English is the official language of Jamaica, residents often use Jamaican Patois, a distinct Creole language. Practicing a few words or utilizing standard Patois pleasantries such as "Wah gwaan?" (What's up?) will demonstrate respect and help you connect with the locals.

Tipping is expected in Montego Bay, particularly at restaurants and for services like as taxi rides, hotel employees, and tour guides. If a service fee has not already been included to your payment, a 10-15% tip is appreciated.

Rastafarianism: Like the rest of Jamaica, Montego Bay has a sizable Rastafarian population. Rastafarianism is a religious and cultural movement with its own set of beliefs and practices. It is critical to observe Rastafarian customs and practices while visiting regions of Rastafarian influence, such as the Rastafari Indigenous Village.

Photography: Always get permission before photographing someone, particularly children or sacred locations. Some residents may not feel comfortable being photographed, so please respect their privacy.

While travelers are typically safe in Montego Bay, it is always vital to be vigilant and aware of your surroundings. Avoid flaunting costly jewelry or valuables, particularly in public places, and use caution while going alone at night.

You may show respect for Jamaican culture, create strong connections with the people, and have a more enjoyable time in Montego Bay by following these local traditions and exercising excellent manners.

Currency and Money Issues

To have a comfortable financial experience when visiting Montego Bay, it is important to get acquainted with the local currency and money problems. Here are some important things to know about currency and money management in Montego Bay:

The Jamaican Dollar (JMD) is the country's official currency. It is good to have some local cash on hand for minor costs and transactions.

Currency Exchange: Major international currencies, such as US dollars, British pounds, or euros, may be exchanged into Jamaican dollars through banks, currency exchange offices, or approved foreign exchange bureaus. To guarantee fair exchange rates, it is suggested that you exchange your money at these official outlets.

While credit and debit cards are generally accepted in Montego Bay, it is best to have extra cash on hand for minor transactions, street sellers, and establishments that may not take cards. Keep smaller amounts on hand for ease of use.

ATMs: There are various ATMs in Montego Bay where you may withdraw Jamaican dollars using your international debit or credit card. Check with your bank to see if there are any foreign transaction fees or currency conversion costs.

Notify Your Bank: Before flying to Montego Bay, notify your bank or credit card provider of your plans to prevent having your cards stopped due to suspicious behavior. It is also beneficial to have your bank's emergency contact number on hand in case you want assistance with your cards.

Currency Rates: Keep up to speed on current currency rates to guarantee you're getting a good bargain when exchanging money. Because exchange rates might vary, it's a good idea to double-check rates before making any currency conversions.

Bargaining and Tipping: Except in certain instances like as buying things from street vendors or artisan fairs, bargaining is not often performed in Montego Bay. However, tipping is typical in places where excellent service is provided, such as restaurants, hotels, and tour guides. Before tipping, check to see whether a service fee has already been included to your account.

Money Safety: As with any trip location, it is critical to keep your money and possessions secure. Passports, extra cash, and other valuables should be stored in hotel safes or secure lockers. To prevent pickpocketing, carry your money in a safe travel wallet or money belt and use caution in busy situations.

Travel Insurance: It is strongly advised to obtain travel insurance that covers medical bills, trip cancellation, and loss or theft of personal possessions. Check that your insurance coverage covers your particular activities and demands while in Montego Bay.

Keep Receipts: Keep receipts for any big purchases or costs, since you may need them for customs clearance when departing Jamaica or for insurance claims.

Understanding the currency and money concerns in Montego Bay will allow you to efficiently manage your funds, make educated choices while converting money, and have a trouble-free vacation.

Emergency Contacts for Users

When visiting Montego Bay, it is essential to have access to emergency contacts in case of an emergency or if you need help. Here are some crucial emergency call numbers to remember:

Contact the Jamaican Constabulary Force by phoning 119 in the event of an emergency or to report a crime.

Ambulance and Medical Emergencies: Dial 119 to seek an ambulance or emergency medical help in the event of a medical emergency. The operator will put you in touch with the necessary medical services.

Fire and Rescue: Dial 110 to call the Jamaica Fire Brigade if you have a fire or need rescue assistance.

Tourist Police in Montego Bay: The Tourist Police can give support and advise to travelers. They can help with problems like missing passports, theft, and general safety concerns. Contact them at +1 (876) 952-0857 or visit their office on Howard Cooke Boulevard at the Montego Bay Police Station.

Embassy or Consulate: If you are a foreign visitor and need help from your country's embassy or consulate, have their contact information handy. Check with your embassy or consulate in Jamaica for contact information and emergency procedures.

Poison Control: Call the National Poison Control Centre at +1 (876) 927-7979 if you or someone you know has consumed anything possibly dangerous.

Roadside help: If your vehicle breaks down or you need roadside help, call your rental car company or a local roadside assistance provider.

Tourist Information: Contact the Jamaica Tourist Board at +1 (876) 929-9200 for general tourist information, queries, or assistance, or visit their website for useful resources.

Hospitals and Medical Facilities: Having contact information for local hospitals and medical facilities is useful in the event of non-emergency medical requirements. Cornwall Regional Hospital and the Montego Bay Hospital are two important hospitals in Montego Bay.

Personal Emergency Contacts: Ensure that you have the contact information for your travel companions, family members, or friends who can help you in the event of a personal emergency.

It is best to store these emergency contacts on your phone or write them down and keep them in a convenient location. To guarantee your safety during your stay to Montego Bay, acquaint yourself with the local emergency protocols and follow any further advise supplied by your hotel or local authorities.

CHAPTER 5

Local Cuisine and Dinning

Overview of Jamaican Cuisine

Jamaican cuisine is distinguished by its bright tastes, distinctive spices, and blend of African, European, Indian, and Chinese influences. Montego Bay cuisine, like that of the rest of Jamaica, provides a delectable variety of meals that represent the island's rich cultural background. Here's a rundown of Jamaican cuisine, with a focus on certain prominent meals and culinary traditions:

Jerk Chicken: Perhaps Jamaica's most renowned dish, jerk chicken is a must-try. It entails marinating chicken in a spice mixture that includes scotch bonnet peppers, allspice, thyme, and other herbs and spices before grilling it to perfection. As a consequence, the chicken is smokey, peppery, and tasty.

Curry Goat: This dish exemplifies Jamaican cuisine's Indian influence. Tender goat flesh is marinated and slow-cooked in a fragrant curry sauce seasoned with turmeric, cumin, coriander, and other spices. It is often eaten with rice and peas, a traditional Jamaican side dish.

Ackee and Saltfish: Ackee and saltfish is a popular breakfast meal in Jamaica and is considered the country's national cuisine. Ackee, a West African fruit, is sautéed with salted codfish, onions, tomatoes, and spices. It's usually accompanied with boiling green bananas, fried plantains, or dumplings.

Escovitch Fish is a famous seafood meal in Jamaica, particularly around the shore. A entire fish is marinated in vinegar, onions, carrots, bell peppers, and scotch bonnet peppers before being fried till crispy. It is often served with festival (sweet fried bread) or bammy (cassava flatbread).

Callaloo is a classic Jamaican vegetable dish prepared with leafy greens such as amaranth or taro leaves. Coconut milk, onions, garlic, scallions, thyme, and other ingredients are cooked with the greens. It may be served as a side dish or as a soup with additions such as okra, crab, or saltfish.

Patties: Jamaican patties are delicious pastry filled with spices ground meat, fowl, or vegetables. The dough is flaky and golden, and the contents are spiced and seasoned with herbs and spices. Patties are a popular snack or lunch alternative for those on the move.

Rice and peas, often known as "Jamaican rice and beans," are a popular side dish. Rice is cooked with kidney beans, coconut milk, scallions, thyme, and sometimes extra ingredients like as garlic and allspice. It is often served with meat or fish meals.

Festival is a traditional Jamaican bread prepared with cornmeal and flour and seasoned with sugar, baking powder, and salt. Deep-frying the dough till brown and somewhat sweet. It's often served as a side dish with jerk chicken, seafood, or other main meals.

Rum: Jamaica is famous for its rum, and trying local rum is a must. The island produces rums that range from light and smooth to rich and full-bodied. Rum is often consumed straight, in cocktails such as the famed Jamaican rum punch, or as a component in cooking and baking.

Tropical Fruits: Due to its location in the Caribbean, Montego Bay has an abundance of tropical fruits. Mangoes, papayas, pineapples, guavas, coconuts, and other fresh and tasty fruits are available. These fruits are often used in refreshing drinks, smoothies, desserts, and as meal accompaniments.

When in Montego Bay, be sure to visit the local restaurants, food booths, and marketplaces to sample the variety and exquisite tastes of Jamaican cuisine.

Must-Try Recipes

There are numerous must-try meals in Montego Bay that demonstrate the vivid tastes and culinary traditions of Jamaican cuisine. Here are a few popular foods that you should try:

Jerk Chicken: This traditional Jamaican meal has marinated chicken in a fiery jerk seasoning combination that includes scotch bonnet peppers, allspice, thyme, garlic, and other fragrant spices. Traditionally, the chicken is roasted over a wood fire, yielding smokey and delicious flesh.

Curry Goat: This tasty and hearty meal exemplifies the Indian influence on Jamaican cuisine. Slow-cooked tender goat meat in a fragrant curry sauce with a variety of spices results in a wonderful and aromatic curry meal. It's usually served with rice and peas.

Ackee and Saltfish: Ackee and saltfish, Jamaica's national cuisine, is a unique blend of ackee fruit and salted codfish. The ackee fruit is sautéed with salted codfish, onions, tomatoes, and spices to make a delicious and flavorful meal that is often served with fried dumplings or boiled green bananas.

Escovitch Fish is a famous seafood meal in Jamaica, especially around the shore. Whole fish, such as snapper, is fried until crispy before being covered with a sour sauce composed of vinegar, onions, carrots, bell peppers, and scotch bonnet peppers. It's a tasty and aesthetically pleasing meal.

Pepper Shrimp: If you like spicy seafood, pepper shrimp is a must-try. Before being sautéed to perfection, fresh shrimp are marinated in a hot combination of spices that includes scotch bonnet chiles, garlic, and other ingredients. It's a delectable and spicy delight.

Oxtail stew is a rich and fragrant meal created from soft oxtail chunks cooked in a savory sauce with spices, onions, tomatoes, and other ingredients. During the lengthy simmering period, the beef becomes wonderfully soft and delicious, resulting in a substantial and fulfilling stew.

Jamaican Patties: Jamaican patties are delicious pastry filled with spices ground meat, poultry, or veggies. The flaky pastry is stuffed with a rich and fragrant filling, making it a popular snack or lunch alternative.

Ital Cuisine: For vegetarian or vegan choices, Jamaican Ital cuisine is worth investigating. Rastafarian ideas affect Italian cuisine, which emphasizes natural and plant-based components. Ingredients such as callaloo, plantains, yams, and coconut milk are often used in dishes that are both tasty and healthful.

Rum Punch: Because Jamaica is known for its rum manufacturing, a refreshing rum punch is a must-try. Rum punch is a wonderful tropical beverage made with Jamaican rum, fruit juices, lime, and spices that embodies the flavor of the island.

Fresh Tropical Fruits: Montego Bay is brimming with tropical fruits. Don't pass up the chance to eat fresh and luscious fruits including mangoes, pineapples, papayas, coconuts, and more. They are not only tasty, but they also provide a sense of the natural wealth of the Caribbean.

These are just a handful of the meals you must eat in Montego Bay. Exploring the local culinary scene will certainly expose you to many more delectable Jamaican specialties.

Montego Bay's Most Popular Restaurants

Montego Bay has a diverse food scene, ranging from simple local restaurants to expensive fine dining venues. Here are some prominent Montego Bay restaurants recognized for their wonderful meals and welcoming atmosphere:

Scotchies: A local and tourist favorite, Scotchies is known for its genuine Jamaican jerk food. They offer delectable jerk chicken, jerk pig, and other grilled specialities, along with traditional sides like festival and roasted breadfruit. The rustic outdoor backdrop enhances the eating experience.

Pier One: Located on a lovely shoreline, Pier One provides a one-of-a-kind dining experience with spectacular bay views. They specialize on seafood and Jamaican cuisine, including items such as grilled lobster, steamed fish, and curry shrimp on the menu. Locals and tourists alike enjoy the live music and lively environment.

The Sugar Mill Restaurant: The Sugar Mill Restaurant, located in the historic Half Moon Resort, offers an exceptional dining experience in a beautifully restored 17th-century sugar mill. The cuisine combines Jamaican and foreign tastes with fresh local ingredients. It is a fantastic option for a special occasion because to the romantic setting and attentive service.

Mystic Thai: If you're wanting Asian cuisines, Mystic Thai in Montego Bay has an amazing range of Thai food. Their menu features classic Thai meals including pad Thai, green curry, and crispy duck, all cooked with premium ingredients and authentic tastes. The warm ambiance and excellent service add to the eating experience.

Marguerite's Seafood by the Sea: Marguerite's Seafood by the Sea, located on the Hip Strip, provides a delightful coastal location with spectacular ocean views. Fresh seafood meals, such as grilled fish, lobster, and shrimp, are their specialty. The romantic setting and tasty seafood delicacies make the restaurant a popular option for a wonderful dining experience.

The Houseboat Grill: This one-of-a-kind restaurant is located in the Montego Bay Marine Park on a floating boat. The Houseboat Grill provides an intimate and pleasant eating experience, as well as a broad cuisine that includes steak, seafood, and vegetarian alternatives. The tranquil setting and great service make it a local and tourist favorite.

The Pelican Grill: The Pelican Grill, which opened in 1964, is a Montego Bay institution. This traditional Jamaican restaurant delivers a combination of foreign and local cuisine, such as grilled steaks, fresh seafood, and Jamaican staples like curry goat. Its vintage appeal and great cuisine make it a popular eating destination.

The Pork Pit: For a relaxed and genuine Jamaican dining experience, visit The Pork Pit. This open-air restaurant is famous for its succulent jerk pork and jerk chicken. You may have your tasty lunch while taking in the vibrant scene at picnic tables.

Hard Rock Café: A worldwide classic, the Hard Rock Café Montego Bay location provides American-style cuisine with a rock 'n' roll ambience. Enjoy traditional burgers, ribs, and other comfort food favorites while seeing music luminaries' memorabilia. The energetic atmosphere is enhanced by live music performances.

Pelican Restaurant: Pelican Restaurant, located at the Montego Bay Yacht Club, provides beachfront dining with an international and Jamaican cuisine. Their broad cuisine includes something for everyone, from marine specialities to spaghetti, salads, and sumptuous desserts. The stunning waterfront views make it a comfortable eating place.

These are just a handful of the prominent restaurants in Montego Bay, reflecting the area's various gastronomic choices. Montego Bay boasts a dining experience to satisfy every pallet, whether you're looking for Jamaican delicacies, foreign cuisine, or seafood pleasures.

CHAPTER 6

Exploring Montego Bay

Hip Strip in Montego Bay

Gloucester Avenue, popularly known as the Montego Bay Hip Strip, is a dynamic and active section of Montego Bay, Jamaica. It is a popular tourist attraction with several alternatives for entertainment, food, shopping, and nightlife. Here's a quick rundown of the Montego Bay Hip Strip:

The Hip Strip is well-known for its entertainment options, which include live music, street performers, and cultural events. Reggae music, dancehall performances, and traditional Jamaican folk music are available to visitors.

Restaurants and Bars: There are various restaurants and bars in the region that provide a wide range of food, from Jamaican cuisines to foreign tastes. Visitors may enjoy the dynamic ambiance while indulging in local favorites like as jerk chicken, seafood, and tropical beverages.

Shopping: With an abundance of stores and boutiques, the Montego Bay Hip Strip is a shopper's dream. Souvenirs, local crafts, clothes, jewelry, and artwork are available to visitors. The Hip Strip Craft Market and the Harbour Street Craft Market are two popular shopping destinations.

Nightlife: With its thriving nightlife scene, the Hip Strip comes alive after dark. There are several pubs, clubs, and lounges where guests may listen to music, dance, and socialize. Some prominent evening entertainment places include Margaritaville, Pier One, and The Brewery.

Beaches: The Hip Strip is flanked with lovely beaches where guests may unwind and soak up the rays. Doctor's Cave Beach is a popular destination in the region, noted for its stunning turquoise seas and white sand. Cornwall Beach and Walter Fletcher Beach are two more neighboring beaches.

Accommodations: The Hip Strip has a variety of lodging options to meet a variety of budgets and interests. Visitors may choose a place to stay within walking distance of the entertainment and sights, ranging from luxury resorts and boutique hotels to budget-friendly guesthouses.

Watersports and Activities: The Hip Strip serves as a center for a variety of watersports and activities. Snorkeling, scuba diving, jet skiing, parasailing, and glass-bottom boat cruises are available to visitors. Water sports providers may be located throughout the strip, providing thrilling experiences for those looking for adventure.

Local Culture: The Montego Bay Hip Strip allows visitors to experience Jamaica's lively local culture. Visitors may meet friendly people, listen to reggae music, and see traditional dance performances.

The Hip Strip is readily accessible and well-connected to the rest of Montego Bay. Taxis, buses, and tour operators may be found along the strip, making it easy for tourists to explore the city's other attractions.

Events and Festivals: The Hip Strip offers a variety of events and festivals throughout the year, including music festivals, culinary festivals, and cultural festivities. These events highlight Jamaica's rich tradition and vibrant character.

The Montego Bay Hip Strip is a must-see for anybody looking for entertainment, eating, shopping, or a taste of Jamaican culture. It has a dynamic and energetic ambiance, making it a great experience for guests throughout their time in Montego Bay.

Purchasing

Visitors to the Montego Bay Hip Strip will discover a broad assortment of stores and marketplaces selling a variety of things, ranging from souvenirs and local crafts to apparel and artwork. Here are some of the Hip Strip's retail highlights:

Hip Strip Craft Market: The Craft Market, located on the Montego Bay Hip Strip, is a popular destination for travellers searching for unique souvenirs and handmade crafts. Woodcarvings, straw baskets, paintings, jewelry, and apparel are among the many local crafts available. Bargaining is widespread at the market, so be prepared to haggle with merchants.

Harbour Street Craft Market: Another popular shopping attraction close is the Harbour Street Craft

Market. It also sells locally manufactured crafts and artwork, such as wood carvings, ceramics, leather products, and textiles. The market allows you to interact with local craftspeople and learn about their trade.

Duty-Free Shopping: Montego Bay is well-known for its duty-free shopping. The Hip Strip is home to various duty-free shops where tourists may purchase luxury things including jewelry, watches, perfumes, and gadgets at tax-free pricing. These establishments often stock globally famous brands and provide consumers with a diverse selection of possibilities.

Local Boutiques: There are a number of boutique businesses along the Hip Strip that sell apparel, swimwear, accessories, and resort wear. These shops cater to both residents and visitors, offering a variety of attractive alternatives for those wishing to renew their holiday wardrobe or locate one-of-a-kind fashion items.

Retail malls: Visitors may explore retail malls around the Hip Strip for a more extensive shopping experience. Two popular possibilities are the Half Moon Shopping Village and the Whitter Village Shopping Centre. These shopping malls have a combination of local and foreign businesses, such as apparel stores, souvenir shops, restaurants, and cafés.

Art Galleries: There are various art galleries in Jamaica that showcase the dynamic and diversified Jamaican art scene. These galleries often exhibit works by local artists, such as paintings, sculptures, and mixed-media pieces. Visitors may discover and acquire artwork that depicts Jamaica's rich cultural history.

Local Cuisine Products: Foodies may also discover businesses offering Jamaican cuisine and spices, enabling them to carry a taste of Jamaica home with them. Look for shops that sell Jamaican coffee, jerk spices, spicy sauces, rum cakes, and other delectable treats.

It is critical to remain cautious of your surroundings and safeguard your stuff while shopping on the Montego Bay Hip Strip. Negotiating pricing is frequent in marketplaces, so don't be afraid to do so, but remember to do it gently. Additionally, before making a purchase, confirm the legitimacy and quality of the item, particularly if it is costly or handcrafted.

Overall, the shopping experience on the Montego Bay Hip Strip combines cultural authenticity with tourist-friendly alternatives, enabling tourists to buy unique gifts, support local craftsmen, and indulge in retail therapy while in Montego Bay.

Bars and Restaurants

When it comes to eating and enjoying a bustling nightlife, the Montego Bay Hip Strip has a wide range of restaurants and bars to suit all interests and inclinations. Here are some highlights of the eating and drinking choices on the Montego Bay Hip Strip, ranging from traditional Jamaican cuisine to foreign cuisines and a busy bar scene:

Jamaican Food

The Pelican Grill: This long-standing Jamaican restaurant is recognized for its delectable Jamaican delicacies such as jerk chicken, curried goat, and shellfish. It provides a relaxed and inviting environment for both residents and visitors.

Scotchies: Scotchies is a prominent Jamaican jerk restaurant noted for its tasty jerk chicken, pig, and seafood. The outdoor environment adds to the real feel.

Cuisine from Around the World:

Margaritaville: A well-known Hip Strip venue, Margaritaville is a vibrant restaurant and bar that serves a variety of foreign foods, including burgers, seafood, and Tex-Mex cuisine. There is also a water slide, a swimming pool, and live entertainment.

Blue Beat Ultra bar: This upscale bar serves a blend of Jamaican and foreign cuisine. It's well-known for its live music, DJ performances, and lively environment.

Seafood:

Pier 1: Pier 1 is a prominent seafood restaurant located on a pier overlooking the ocean that serves a range of fresh seafood meals. In the nights, it also changes into a bustling nightclub with live music and DJs.

The Houseboat Grill: This unusual restaurant specializes in seafood and steak dishes and is located on a moored houseboat. It is a popular option for special occasions because to its beautiful location and sea views.

Nightlife & Nightclubs:

Margaritaville has a busy bar scene with themed evenings, live music, and a party atmosphere in addition to its food. It's a fantastic spot for tropical drinks and dancing the night away.

The Brewery: Known for its extensive assortment of craft beers, The Brewery provides a casual and welcoming atmosphere. It also offers pub meals and features live music events on occasion.

Coral Cliff Gaming Lounge: A casino, sports bar, and live music venue are all part of this entertainment complex. Visitors may play video games, watch sports, and listen to local musicians.

Cafés and Fast Food Restaurants:

Pelican Beach Terrace: This seaside café provides a casual eating experience with sandwiches, salads, and Jamaican delicacies on the menu. It's a nice area to unwind and take in the scenery.

Groovy Grouper Beach Bar & restaurant: This beachfront bar and restaurant on Doctor's Cave Beach has a laid-back feel with a menu that includes burgers, wraps, and seafood.

Please keep in mind that restaurant and bar availability varies, and it's usually a good idea to verify their opening hours and make reservations, particularly during high seasons. The Montego Bay Hip Strip has a vibrant and varied eating and bar scene, guaranteeing that guests may find something to their liking and have a wonderful gastronomic experience.

Entertainment at Night

The Montego Bay Hip Strip is well-known for its bustling and active nightlife scene, which provides a wide range of alternatives for people looking for entertainment, dancing, and mingling when the sun goes down. Here are some of the nightlife highlights on the Montego Bay Hip Strip:

Dancehalls and clubs:

Margaritaville is a famous daytime venue that changes into a vibrant nightclub in the nights. It has a dance floor, live DJs, and special evenings, all of which contribute to the exciting party atmosphere.

Pier 1: Pier 1 is a renowned nightclub noted for its vibrant environment and numerous live performances. It is located on a pier overlooking the lake. It organizes themed events with music ranging from reggae and dancehall to hip-hop and soca, such as Reggae Nights and Latin Nights.

Beach Gatherings:

Doctor's Cave Beach Party: This beach party, held at Doctor's Cave Beach, provides a one-of-a-kind experience of dancing and mingling beneath the stars. Live music, DJs, beach bonfires, and a vibrant atmosphere are all part of the celebration.

Gaming and Casinos:

Coral Cliff Gaming club: Coral Cliff is a prominent gaming club on the Hip Strip that features casino games, live entertainment, and a sports bar. Visitors may try their luck at numerous gaming tables and slot machines while sipping cocktails and listening to live music.

Performing Live Music:

The Blue Beat Ultra Lounge has live music performances ranging from reggae and jazz to soul and R&B. It provides an intimate location in which to enjoy superb live music while sipping beverages.

Margaritaville: In addition to its nightclub environment, Margaritaville often has live music performances, including local bands and DJs, which adds to the lively atmosphere.

Sports Pubs:

The Brewery: Known for its specialty brews, The Brewery also has a sports bar section where guests may have a drink while watching live sports events on huge screens. It has a laid-back vibe and sometimes has live music.

Karaoke Parties:

Several clubs and lounges on the Hip Strip organize karaoke nights, enabling guests to show off their singing abilities while having a pleasant evening of entertainment.

Festivals and street parties:

The Montego Bay Hip Strip is well-known for its street parties and festivals, particularly during holidays and special occasions. These events often include live music, food vendors, and a vibrant ambiance.

Going to the bar:

The Hip Strip has a range of clubs and lounges within walking distance, making it perfect for bar hopping and discovering new places. Visitors may wander from one pub to the next, experiencing various atmospheres, music styles, and drink selections.

It's worth noting that the nightlife scene on the Montego Bay Hip Strip may become a little rowdy and congested, particularly on weekends and during peak tourist season. Visitors should exercise caution, protect their things, and limit their alcohol intake. Check the particular events and timetables of venues ahead of time to guarantee a memorable and pleasurable night out on the town.

Doctor's Cave Beach

Doctor's Cave Beach is a well-known and attractive beach on Jamaica's Montego Bay Hip Strip. It has received worldwide acclaim for its crystal-clear turquoise seas, powdered white sand, and peaceful atmosphere. Here's a quick rundown of what makes Doctor's Cave Beach a must-see:

Doctor's Cave Beach is magnificent in its natural beauty. The fine, white sand is ideal for sunbathing and relaxation. The seas are very clean, making snorkeling and swimming quite enjoyable.

Swimming and Snorkeling: Doctor's Cave Beach's quiet and welcoming waters make it great for swimming. The beach has dedicated swimming areas for both adults and children. Snorkelers may explore the bright underwater environment, which is rich in coral reefs and marine life.

Beach Facilities: Doctor's Cave Beach offers guests with handy amenities such as beach chairs and umbrellas for hire. For extra comfort and convenience, there are also changing rooms, showers, and restrooms.

Watersports Activities: Doctor's Cave Beach has a variety of watersports activities for those looking for excitement. Jet skiing, parasailing, kayaking, and paddleboarding are among the activities available to visitors. Visitors may have exhilarating adventures on the water thanks to the availability of equipment rental services.

Beachfront Dining: There are various beachfront restaurants and bars along the beach where tourists may enjoy excellent meals and cool drinks while admiring the breathtaking views. It's an excellent chance to sample authentic Jamaican food and tropical beverages.

Doctor's Cave Beach has an interesting history. It was named after a well-known British osteopath who felt the beach's waters were restorative. The beach became a popular location for travelers looking for its claimed restorative properties, despite the fact that the claims of its healing abilities have not been scientifically substantiated.

Beach Club Membership: Beach club membership at Doctor's Cave Beach allows exclusive access to a secluded portion of the beach, reserved lounge chairs, and extra facilities. Members get access to a more private and customized beach experience.

Nearby Attractions: Doctor's Cave Beach is conveniently positioned among other renowned Montego Bay attractions. The Hip Strip, with its shopping, eating, and entertainment choices, is open to visitors. In addition, attractions such as the Montego Bay Marine Park, Cornwall Beach, and the Montego Bay Yacht Club are nearby.

Doctor's Cave Beach holds a variety of events and festivals throughout the year, including beach parties, live music performances, and cultural festivities. These activities bring excitement and enjoyment to the beach experience.

Doctor's Cave Beach is readily accessible since it is just a short distance from the Montego Bay International Airport. Many hotels and resorts along the Hip Strip are within walking distance, making it a handy option for a day trip or a peaceful beach retreat.

Doctor's Cave Beach provides a wonderful beach experience in Montego Bay, whether you're looking for a quiet day of sunbathing, thrilling watersports experiences, or just a serene vacation surrounded by natural beauty.

Rose Hall Great House

The Rose Hall Great House, situated in Montego Bay, Jamaica, is a historic and landmark palace. It is well-known for its rich history, enthralling stories, and breathtaking architecture. Here's a rundown of what makes the Rose Hall Great House a must-see:

Historical Importance: The Rose Hall Great House is an important part of Jamaican history. It was constructed in the late 18th century as a reminder of the island's colonial heritage and the sugar plantation period. Annie Palmer, the fabled "White Witch" who resided there and is a major character in local mythology, is commemorated by the house's name.

Architectural Wonder: The Great House is an outstanding example of Georgian architecture. It has graceful lines, vast rooms, and lovely colonial-style furniture. Visitors may tour the many rooms, including the bedrooms, dining room, and living spaces, and observe the period workmanship and architectural elements.

Tales and Ghost Stories: There are many interesting tales and ghost stories surrounding the Rose Hall Great House. According to local legend, Annie Palmer, who possessed the mansion in the early nineteenth century, practiced witchcraft and was known for her harshness. Many stories surround her life and tragic death, giving an intriguing and frightening touch to the history of the Great House.

Guided Tours: Visitors to the Rose Hall Great House may enjoy guided tours lead by qualified guides who share insights into its history and mythology. The tours take visitors on a fascinating trip around the home, revealing anecdotes about its past occupants and the events that occurred inside its walls.

Historic displays: The Great House has displays that highlight the region's history and cultural heritage. Visitors may learn about the sugar plantation history, enslaved people's life, and the effect of colonialism in Jamaica. These displays provide a more in-depth knowledge of the time's social and economic background.

Beautiful Gardens and Grounds: The Rose Hall Great House is surrounded by beautiful tropical gardens and well-kept grounds. Visitors may walk around the gardens, taking in the brilliant flowers, towering palm palms, and peaceful environment. The vistas of the surrounding countryside and the Caribbean Sea add to the experience's allure.

Night Tours: The Rose Hall Great House provides night tours for those looking for a more adventurous experience. These tours let you to explore the home after dark, adding an added sense of intrigue to your stay. The darkly lighted chambers and spooky stories create a chilling atmosphere.

Events and Weddings: The Rose Hall Great House is available for a variety of events and weddings. Its grandeur and historical importance make it a one-of-a-kind and unforgettable setting for special events. Visitors may ask about organizing events or visiting one of the Great House's numerous cultural and musical activities.

The Rose Hall Great House offers a gift store where tourists may buy souvenirs, local crafts, and publications about Jamaican history and culture. On-site, there is also a restaurant serving traditional Jamaican food and cool refreshments.

Accessibility: The Rose Hall Great House is situated roughly 15 minutes by vehicle from Montego Bay. It is a popular destination for travelers staying in Montego Bay and other adjacent locations, since it provides a view into Jamaica's history as well as the opportunity to investigate its interesting mythology.

A tour to the Rose Hall Great House immerses you in Jamaica's history, architecture, and enthralling mythology. The Great House provides a unique and fascinating adventure in Montego Bay, whether you're interested in the colonial past, captivated by ghost tales, or just admire gorgeous architecture.

Croydon Plantation

Croydon estate is a beautiful and historic estate in Jamaica's Catadupa Mountains, near Montego Bay. It provides tourists with a once-in-a-lifetime chance to tour a functioning plantation, learn about Jamaica's agricultural tradition, and take in the natural beauty of the region. The following are the highlights of a visit to Croydon Plantation:

Croydon Plantation is located in the picturesque Catadupa Mountains, offering spectacular vistas of lush foliage, rolling hills, and flowing waterfalls. The farm is surrounded by tropical trees, which creates a peaceful and relaxing ambiance.

Croydon Plantation offers guided tours given by professional guides who impart insights into the plantation's history, culture, and agricultural processes. The excursions provide an opportunity to learn about Jamaica's unique plants, fruits, and spices, as well as the plantation's importance in the island's agricultural economy.

Fruit Tasting: The ability to indulge in a fruit tasting experience is one of the attractions of a visit to Croydon Plantation. Guests may try tropical fruits cultivated on the farm, such as pineapple, mango, jackfruit, guava, and others. It's an opportunity to appreciate the flavors of Jamaica's abundant vegetables.

Croydon Plantation is well-known for its coffee output. Visitors may join a coffee tour to learn about the cultivation, harvesting, and roasting of coffee beans. The trip includes a tasting session during which visitors may try several coffee varietals and enjoy their rich flavors and smells.

Spice Garden: The estate has a spice garden where visitors may learn about the fragrant herbs and spices that go into Jamaican cuisine. Guides explain the applications and qualities of numerous spices like as cinnamon, nutmeg, allspice, and ginger, allowing visitors to get an understanding of the island's culinary heritage.

Nature Walks: Croydon Plantation provides nature walks for tourists to enjoy the natural beauty of the surrounding region. The pathways run through tropical woods, beside flowing streams, and among a variety of flora and wildlife. It's a chance to take in the fresh air, peace, and plenty of animals.

Visitors are given to a traditional Jamaican barbeque meal as part of their plantation experience. The lunch often consists of succulent jerk chicken, roasted pork, fresh salads, and regional side dishes. It's an opportunity to sample traditional Jamaican tastes in a beautiful outdoor environment.

Trip to a nearby waterfall, where visitors may cool off in the delightful natural pools: Croydon Plantation provides an optional trip to a nearby waterfall, where visitors can cool off in the pleasant natural pools. The waterfall is a hidden jewel surrounded by thick foliage that offers a peaceful respite from the heat.

Visitors may explore and buy a variety of local items, including coffee, spices, fruit preserves, and handcrafted crafts, in the plantation's gift store. It's a chance to bring home a piece of Jamaica's agricultural legacy while also supporting local artists.

Croydon Plantation provides an informative and family-friendly experience that is appropriate for guests of all ages. Children may learn about agricultural operations, engage with farm animals, and take part in educational and entertaining activities.

Croydon Plantation offers a revitalizing and engaging experience in Jamaica's countryside. A visit to Croydon Plantation gives a unique view into Jamaica's rich cultural and natural legacy, whether you're interested in agriculture, love exploring nature, or just want to revel in the island's delicacies.

Rafting on the Martha Brae River

Martha Brae River Rafting is a famous and beautiful destination near Montego Bay, Jamaica. It provides tourists with a quiet and gorgeous river rafting experience, enabling them to float down the Martha Brae River on bamboo rafts. Here's what you may anticipate if you go rafting on the Martha Brae River:

Bamboo Rafts: Your river adventure starts when you board a traditional bamboo raft, which is piloted by a trained and experienced raft captain. Handcrafted from bamboo poles, these rafts provide a rustic and genuine method to cross the river.

Waters that are tranquil and Serene: The Martha Brae River is famed for its tranquil and crystal-clear waters. You'll be surrounded by thick tropical greenery, towering trees, and vivid flora as you float along, providing a quiet and attractive scene.

Raft Captains with Knowledge: Raft captains are not only excellent at managing the rafts, but they are also knowledgeable guides. They add to the whole experience by providing insightful comments on the river, its history, and the surrounding ecology.

Relaxation and scenic views: Martha Brae River Rafting provides a tranquil and leisurely experience that allows you to relax and appreciate the natural beauty that surrounds you. The river's calm current sweeps you along, giving you plenty of time to soak in the spectacular vistas, snap photographs, and savor the peacefulness of the surroundings.

Flora and animals: The river is home to a wide variety of flora and animals. You may see several bird types, butterflies, and maybe a peek of river fauna as you glide along. The raft captains are experts at pointing out the many flora and animals that live in the river.

Martha Brae River Rafting is often viewed as a romantic activity, making it a popular option for couples. The romantic ambience created by the gorgeous backdrop, gentle swaying of the raft, and tranquil environment is ideal for couples wishing to make lasting memories.

Riverbank Attractions: There are attractive thatched-roof gazebos along the riverbanks where you may stop for a refreshing drink or shop local crafts and souvenirs. These pauses allow you to stretch your legs, connect with people, and immerse yourself in Jamaica's unique culture.

River Dipping: You may have the chance to take a relaxing dip in the river while rafting. Your raft captain may direct you to a safe and appropriate location where you can swim in the calm waters of the Martha Brae River, making the trip much more enjoyable.

Riverbank Massage: As an optional extra, some Martha Brae River Rafting programs include a peaceful riverbank massage. This helps you to relax even more as you enjoy a pleasant massage while listening to the calming sounds of the river.

Martha Brae River Rafting is accessible and family-friendly to people of all ages and physical abilities. The river's mild flow and solid bamboo rafts make it a safe and pleasurable experience for families, couples, and lone tourists alike.

Martha Brae River Rafting provides a tranquil and delightful retreat from the hustle and bustle of daily life, enabling you to reconnect with nature, relax, and immerse yourself in the majesty of the Martha Brae River. It's an activity that blends natural beauties with Jamaican warmth, making it a memorable complement to your vacation to Montego Bay.

Montego Bay Marine Park

The Montego Bay Marine Park is a marine park off the coast of Montego Bay, Jamaica. It is a refuge for marine life and allows tourists to explore and enjoy the beauty of Jamaica's underwater environment. Here's what to anticipate if you travel to Montego Bay Marine Park:

Coral Reefs: The marine park is home to robust and diversified coral reefs that are among Jamaica's healthiest. These reefs offer refuge and food for a broad range of marine animals, making it a snorkeling and scuba diving paradise.

Snorkeling is a popular pastime for tourists to the Montego Bay Marine Park. Put on your snorkeling gear and explore the shallow reefs, where you may see colorful fish, delicate corals, and other intriguing sea animals. The crystal-clear waters provide for exceptional vision, enabling you to completely enjoy the underwater environment.

Scuba Diving: The Montego Bay Marine Park provides fascinating scuba diving chances for more experienced divers. There are several diving locations to discover, each with its own distinct characteristics such as cliffs, canyons, and swim-throughs. Divers may see rays, eels, turtles, and schools of tropical fish, among other marine life.

Marine Life: There is an abundance of marine life in the marine park. Aside from the vivid coral reefs, you could see parrotfish, angelfish, butterflyfish, and other species. Larger marine species such as barracudas and nurse sharks may also be seen in the park.

Mangrove Forests: Mangrove forests are important habitats for coastal protection and fish nursery grounds in the Montego Bay Marine Park. You may kayak or take a boat trip through these mangrove environments, witnessing the unique plant and animal life that flourishes in these coastal wetlands.

Educational Programs: The Montego Bay Marine Park provides educational programs and activities to promote marine conservation. Visitors may attend guided tours and interactive workshops to learn about the significance of marine ecosystem preservation and the actions being done to safeguard them.

Glass-Bottom Boat trips: Glass-bottom boat trips are offered if you want to remain dry while admiring the underwater delights. These trips provide a view into the underwater world, enabling you to watch the vibrant coral reefs and marine life from the comfort of a boat.

The Montego Bay Marine Park is committed to fostering environmental awareness and sustainable practices. Visitors are asked to adhere to proper snorkeling and diving practices, such as avoiding touching or destroying coral and respecting marine creatures and their ecosystems.

law for Fishing and Boating: The marine park has laws in place to safeguard the marine ecosystem. To protect the fish population and maintain sustainable fishing methods, several regions have been declared as no-fishing zones. Boaters are also asked to adhere to standards in order to protect coral reefs and other vulnerable areas.

Conservation activities: The Montego Bay Marine Park actively participates in conservation activities, like as coral reef restoration and continuing population monitoring of marine animals. Visitors may help by becoming involved in volunteer activities or giving a gift to the marine park.

A visit to the Montego Bay Marine Park provides a once-in-a-lifetime chance to see Jamaica's underwater treasures. Whether you like snorkeling, scuba diving, or just admire the beauty of marine ecosystems, the Montego Bay Marine Park promises a wonderful and instructive experience.

Montego Bay Cultural Centre

The Montego Bay Cultural Centre is a thriving cultural and historical institution in Montego Bay, Jamaica. It serves as a focal point for the promotion and preservation of Jamaican art, history, and culture.

Here's what to anticipate when you travel to the Montego Bay Cultural Centre:

Exhibits in the Museum: The Cultural Centre has a museum with exhibits on Jamaican history, art, and culture. Artifacts, pictures, artwork, and interactive displays give insights into the island's rich legacy and contributions to the globe.

Historical Exhibits: The museum provides an insight into Montego Bay's past, emphasizing its importance as a historic port town and trading hub. Visitors may learn about the city's colonial past, slavery and emancipation, and the growth of the local economy and industry.

Art Gallery: The Cultural Centre has an art gallery that exhibits the works of renowned and developing local artists. The gallery exhibits paintings, sculptures, ceramics, and mixed-media works in a variety of creative styles and materials. It provides a venue for artists to express themselves and for tourists to admire Jamaican art.

Musical, dance, and theatrical performances are held on a regular basis at the Montego Bay Cultural Centre. Visitors may see live performances of Jamaican music's exuberant rhythms, traditional folk dances, and dramatic shows that dive into the island's cultural heritage.

Workshops and courses: The Cultural Centre provides workshops and courses that allow visitors to interact directly with Jamaican culture. Sessions on traditional Jamaican cookery, drumming, dancing, and even language courses are available. It's an opportunity to acquire new skills and obtain a better knowledge of Jamaican customs.

Special Events and Festivals: Throughout the year, the Cultural Centre hosts a variety of special events and festivals. Art exhibits, cultural festivals, craft fairs, and performances by prominent local and worldwide artists are examples of such events. Participating in these events provides a vibrant and immersive experience in Jamaican culture and entertainment.

The Cultural Centre contains a gift store where tourists may buy a variety of Jamaican-made souvenirs, crafts, artwork, and literature. It's a chance to support local artists while also bringing a bit of Jamaican culture home with you.

The Cultural Centre has a café or restaurant where tourists may enjoy Jamaican food and beverages. It's an ideal location for unwinding, recharging, and savoring the delicacies of the island while immersing yourself in the cultural ambiance.

Interactive Displays: To improve the tourist experience, the Cultural Centre features interactive displays and multimedia presentations. These interactive components enable visitors to interact with the exhibits and learn about Jamaican culture in a hands-on and immersive manner.

Community Engagement: The Montego Bay Cultural Centre regularly interacts with the local community by providing cultural awareness and participation events and activities. It is a meeting space for artists, historians, educators, and people of the community to cooperate, exchange information, and celebrate Jamaican culture.

The Montego Bay Cultural Centre provides an enthralling and engaging experience for tourists interested in Jamaican art, history, and culture. The Cultural Centre gives a window into the complex tapestry of Jamaican past, whether you want to explore the museum displays, watch cultural events, or participate in seminars.

CHAPTER 7

What to Do in Montego Bay (Outdoor Activities)

Park and Dunn's River Falls

Dunn's River Falls and Park is one of Jamaica's most prominent tourist sites, situated in Ocho Rios, about 90 minutes from Montego Bay. Visitors may trek up a series of tiered waterfalls, surrounded by lush flora and breathtaking vistas, at this natural marvel. Here's a rundown of Dunn's River Falls and Park:

The Falls: Dunn's River Falls is a flowing cascade that stretches for around 180 meters (600 ft). It has a succession of natural terraces and ponds that enable tourists to climb from the bottom to the top of the falls while holding hands in a human chain. The cold, refreshing water and beautiful environment make it an unforgettable excursion for people of all ages.

Guided Tours: Guided tours are provided at Dunn's River Falls to guarantee safety and improve the experience. Guides take parties up the falls, offering advice and aid along the route. They provide fascinating insights into the falls' history, geology, and importance, making the visit both instructive and enjoyable.

Climbing the Falls: Climbing Dunn's River Falls is a thrilling and involved experience. Visitors may feel the force of the flowing water as they negotiate the terraces, gripping the rocks with their hands and feet and moving higher. Because the guides give assistance and assure everyone's safety, the climb is appropriate for both experienced hikers and those who are less physically active.

Natural Pools: Several natural pools generated by the waterfall's cascades may be found along the route. These pools allow you to enjoy refreshing swims and rest in the clean, calm water. The pools provide breathtaking views of the surrounding tropical nature and are ideal for shooting great photos.

Dunn's River Falls is hidden amid a tropical jungle, providing a beautiful natural backdrop. A tranquil and scenic ambiance is created by the lush vegetation, bright flowers, and exotic species. As they ascend the falls, visitors may take in the grandeur of the surrounds, making the experience even more unforgettable.

Beach Access: Dunn's River Falls is next to a lovely white sandy beach. After the climb, guests may rest on the beach, sunbathe, swim in the calm Caribbean seas, or participate in water sports. The beach is an ideal area to relax and take in the magnificent coastline views.

Amenities and Facilities: Dunn's River Falls and Park is well-equipped with amenities to improve the comfort and pleasure of visitors. Restrooms, changing rooms, and locker rentals are provided. There are also restaurants and food sellers inside the park where tourists may taste authentic Jamaican cuisine.

Souvenir Shopping: There are various stores and craft markets in the park where tourists may explore and buy gifts like as locally created handicrafts, artwork, apparel, and jewelry. It's a chance to bring home a bit of Jamaican culture while also supporting local artists.

Cultural Performances: Dunn's River Falls hosts live performances of Jamaican music and dance on occasion. Traditional Jamaican cultural acts, such as reggae music, drumming, and folk dances, may be seen by visitors, providing a colorful and joyful flavor to the whole experience.

Dunn's River Falls and Park is dedicated to environmental protection and sustainable tourism. They aggressively encourage tourists to be responsibly, such as not littering and protecting the natural beauty of the falls and surrounding region.

Dunn's River Falls and Park provide a one-of-a-kind and thrilling experience for Montego Bay tourists. Climbing the falls, swimming in natural pools, and relaxing in the beautiful environs make it a must-see sight in Jamaica. Dunn's River Falls & Park provides something for everyone, whether you're looking for adventure, leisure, or cultural enrichment.

Chukka Caribbean Adventures

Chukka Caribbean Adventures is a well-known adventure tour operator in Jamaica, providing tourists to Montego Bay and other prominent areas on the island with a variety of exhilarating activities and excursions. Chukka Caribbean Adventures is noted for its high-quality service, safety standards, and dedication to sustainable tourism, with an emphasis on giving unique experiences in Jamaica's natural environments. Chukka Caribbean Adventures and some of the fascinating activities they provide are described below:

Canopy Zipline Excursions: Chukka Caribbean Adventures is well-known for their thrilling zipline canopy excursions. Visitors may zipline over the trees, taking in stunning views of the beautiful forest, rivers, and waterfalls below. Trained guides assure safety while also providing fascinating information about the area's ecology and animals.

ATV and Dune Buggy trips: Chukka Caribbean Adventures' ATV and dune buggy trips take adventurers on exhilarating off-road experiences. Explore tough terrains, negotiate mud puddles, and locate hidden jewels while feeling the exhilaration of driving these powerful vehicles.

Riding a Horse: Riding a horse allows you to enjoy the beauty of Jamaica's countryside. Chukka Caribbean Adventures provides guided horseback riding experiences through gorgeous paths, pristine beaches, and even into the warm Caribbean Sea with your horse for a delightful dip.

River Tubing: Take an inflatable tube down one of Jamaica's picturesque rivers. Float along the mild currents, take in the scenery, and let the river transport you through beautiful landscapes and dramatic rapids.

Catamaran and Boat trips: Chukka Caribbean Adventures offers catamaran and boat trips that enable guests to see Jamaica's beautiful coastline. Sail over the turquoise seas, snorkel amid the beautiful coral reefs, and unwind on gorgeous beaches under the warm Caribbean sun.

River Rafting: Take a relaxing river rafting trip through Jamaica's gorgeous rivers. Relax on a bamboo raft while a knowledgeable guide navigates the river, offering local history and pointing out noteworthy spots along the route.

Jeep Safari: Take a Jeep safari excursion into the heart of Jamaica's countryside. Explore off-the-beaten-path sights such as secret waterfalls and gorgeous views as you travel through difficult terrain and rural settlements.

Chukka Caribbean Adventures also provides cultural experiences that give insights into Jamaican history, music, and food. Participate in participatory drumming sessions, master traditional dancing skills, or sample genuine Jamaican delicacies during a farm-to-table cooking class.

Combine the thrill of ziplining with a relaxing dip in a natural river pool. The Zip and Dip excursion from Chukka Caribbean Adventures lets you to zip under the forest canopy before cooling yourself in the crystal-clear waters of a remote river.

Chukka Caribbean Adventures is devoted to conserving Jamaica's natural resources and supports a variety of environmental conservation activities. They emphasize responsible tourism and work hard to reduce their environmental effect.

Chukka Caribbean Adventures provides a variety of exhilarating activities for adventure seekers, wildlife lovers, and those wishing to explore Jamaica's beauty and culture. Chukka Caribbean Adventures assures that each tour is a memorable and safe experience by using skilled guides, high-quality equipment, and a commitment to client happiness.

Riding a Horse

Horseback riding is a popular pastime in Montego Bay and across Jamaica, enabling tourists to explore the gorgeous landscapes and enjoy the island's beauty from a different angle. Horseback riding trips allow you to connect with nature while riding through gorgeous paths and even swimming in the warm Caribbean Sea. Here's a rundown of equestrian riding options in Montego Bay:

Riding Experience: Montego Bay horseback riding trips cater to riders of all ability levels, from beginners to expert equestrians. There are alternatives available to fit your comfort and skill level, whether you are a beginning rider or an experienced horse aficionado. The horses on the trips are normally well-trained and well-cared-for, and they are familiar with the local terrain.

Horseback riding trips in Montego Bay take you on magnificent pathways that meander through lush tropical landscapes, stunning slopes, and even along pristine beaches. The paths provide beautiful views of the Caribbean Sea, neighboring mountains, and Jamaica's colorful flora and wildlife.

Beach Rides: Riding along the beach and even swimming with your horse in the water is one of the joys of horseback riding in Montego Bay. Feel the rush as you gallop over the sandy coastlines, taking in the sea wind and the sound of breaking waves.

Horseback riding excursions in Montego Bay emphasise safety and give competent guides with experience managing horses and directing riders of all abilities. The guides give training on horse handling, verify correct helmet and other safety equipment fitting, and provide support and direction during the ride.

Cultural and Historical Insight: Some Montego Bay horseback riding trips include cultural and historical features that provide insights into the local history and customs. You may be able to tour historical places, learn about Jamaican history, and even connect with local people.

Sunset Rides: Consider a sunset horseback riding excursion for a romantic and enchanting experience. As the sun sets over the Caribbean Sea, it casts a golden light over the landscape, creating a wonderfully unforgettable and beautiful ambiance.

Horseback riding experiences in Montego Bay are often ideal for the whole family, including youngsters. Pony rides or shorter, gentler rides that cater exclusively to young riders are provided for children.

Opportunity for Photography: The picturesque splendor of Montego Bay gives several opportunity for breathtaking images throughout your horseback riding excursion. You'll have lots of opportunity to create memories, from sweeping vistas of the coastline to candid photographs of you riding down the beach.

Horseback riding is considered an eco-friendly activity since it allows you to enjoy the natural surroundings without harming the environment. The excursions often follow responsible tourism methods and emphasize the horses' well-being and care.

Relaxation & Nature Connection: Horseback riding in Montego Bay provides an opportunity to unplug from the rush and bustle of everyday life and reconnect with nature. You may appreciate the tranquillity of the surroundings, listen to the sounds of nature, and feel a feeling of calm and serenity as you ride along the gorgeous routes.

Horseback riding in Montego Bay is a fantastic opportunity to immerse yourself in the region's natural beauty, enjoy the excitement of riding, and create lasting memories of your stay in Jamaica. It's an activity for riders of all ages and ability levels, with skilled guides, well-trained horses, and magnificent terrain.

Canopy and Zipline Tours

In Montego Bay, ziplining and canopy excursions provide exciting and daring experiences that enable guests to fly over the trees while taking in spectacular views of the surrounding natural surroundings. Ziplining and canopy trips are ideal for anyone looking for an adrenaline rush and a new view of Montego Bay's splendor. Here's a rundown of Montego Bay ziplining and canopy tours:

Zipline Courses: There are many zipline courses in Montego Bay, which consist of a succession of hanging wires and platforms. These courses are meant to take you on an exciting adventure into the tropical rainforest canopy. Each zipline is made out of a cable strung between two platforms that allows people to zip from one to the other while being tethered to the cable.

Ziplining provides a unique vantage point from which to experience Montego Bay's natural beauty. You'll receive a bird's-eye view of the lush flora, tumbling waterfalls, and distant mountain ranges as you fly through the skies. It's a chance to observe the scenery from a completely different angle.

Canopy Walkways: Canopy tours typically incorporate suspended walkways or sky bridges that link platforms amid the trees, in addition to ziplines. These paths enable you to meander through the canopy, immersing yourself in the natural environment and seeing the rich flora and wildlife up close.

Ziplining is an amazing sport that provides an adrenaline rush as you glide through the air at tremendous speeds. The sensation of weightlessness combined with the pure pleasure of zooming from platform to platform creates an unparalleled trip that will get your pulse racing.

Zipline and canopy tour companies stress safety and give participants with appropriate safety equipment, such as harnesses, helmets, and gloves. Guides are on hand to verify that all safety standards are followed and to help participants during the trip.

Ziplining and canopy trips are typically appropriate for participants of all ages and fitness levels. However, check with individual operators about any age or weight limits that may apply. To guarantee the safety and pleasure of all participants, certain trips may have minimum age or weight limits.

Environmental Education: Many Montego Bay zipline and canopy tour providers include an educational component in their trips. Guides often give information on the area ecology, plants, and animals, enabling guests to learn about the region's different ecosystems.

Ziplining and canopy excursions are ideal for parties and families because they give a shared experience full of thrill and adventure. Whether you're traveling with friends, family, or coworkers, ziplining enables you to make unforgettable experiences.

Opportunity for Photography: Ziplining and canopy excursions provide wonderful opportunity for breathtaking images. Some operators let participants to carry cameras or give designated picture stops throughout the route, ensuring that your memories of soaring through the skies are preserved.

Many zipline and canopy tour businesses in Montego Bay are dedicated to sustainable tourism principles. They value environmental preservation and contribute to local conservation initiatives. Participating in these trips allows you to support ethical and environmentally friendly tourist efforts.

Ziplining and canopy excursions in Montego Bay provide an amazing opportunity to enjoy the region's natural beauty while meeting your adventure appetite. Ziplining and canopy excursions give an exciting adventure in the center of Jamaica's beautiful surroundings, whether you're looking for an adrenaline rush, magnificent panoramic views, or an educational encounter.

Snorkeling and Scuba Diving

Snorkeling and scuba diving at Montego Bay provide fantastic opportunity to experience the Caribbean Sea's rich underwater ecosystem. Montego Bay is a snorkeler and scuba diver's dream, with crystal-clear seas, beautiful coral reefs, and a rich variety of marine life. Here's a rundown of the snorkeling and scuba diving options in Montego Bay:

Snorkeling is a popular hobby that enables you to see the underwater beauty without requiring any training or equipment. You may explore the shallow reefs and see the interesting marine creatures up close with only a mask, snorkel, and fins. Montego Bay has various snorkeling areas with calm seas and diverse wildlife.

Scuba Diving: Scuba diving is an excellent alternative for a more immersive experience. Certified divers may explore the magnificent dive sites of Montego Bay, which include shallow reefs, deeper cliffs, and even submerged shipwrecks. Divers at Montego Bay may expect to see beautiful coral formations, tropical fish, rays, eels, and even turtles and dolphins.

Dive facilities: There are respectable dive facilities in Montego Bay that provide scuba diving training for novices as well as guided dives for certified divers. These facilities have the essential equipment, competent instructors, and safety standards in place to provide a safe and fun diving experience.

Coral Reefs: Montego Bay is home to lush, life-filled coral reefs. Snorkelers and divers may explore these underwater habitats, which are home to a diverse range of hard and soft corals, sponges, and marine organisms. Prepare to see a rainbow of colors and meet a wide range of species, including parrotfish, angelfish, butterflyfish, and many more.

Marine Life: The seas around Montego Bay are teeming with a rich array of marine life. Tropical fish, sea turtles, stingrays, moray eels, lobsters, and even nurse sharks may be encountered by snorkelers and divers. The marine habitat of Montego Bay is a haven for underwater photographers and nature lovers.

PADI Certification: If you aren't already a qualified diver and wish to explore the deeper depths of Montego Bay's underwater environment, consider getting your PADI certification. Several dive facilities in the region provide certification classes where you may obtain the skills and information required to become a certified diver.

Snorkel and Dive trips: Many Montego Bay tour companies provide snorkel and dive trips to the greatest underwater spots in the vicinity. These trips often include transportation, rental equipment, skilled guides, and, in some cases, refreshments or meals. A hassle-free and pleasurable snorkeling or diving experience is ensured by joining an organized expedition.

Night Diving: For qualified divers searching for a one-of-a-kind adventure, Montego Bay offers night diving. Witness the underwater environment shift as nocturnal species come to life, revealing a new viewpoint on the marine ecology.

Dive Safety: When snorkeling or scuba diving, it is critical to prioritize safety. Make sure you have the proper training, follow the diving center's requirements, and always dive with a partner. Respect the marine environment by not touching or harming corals and by never disturbing or chasing marine creatures.

Conservation activities: To safeguard its coral reefs and marine biodiversity, Montego Bay is actively engaged in marine conservation activities. Some diving facilities and organizations provide educational programs and activities to promote awareness about the need of marine ecosystem preservation. Choose ecologically conscientious operators and use ethical snorkeling and diving skills to help their efforts.

Snorkeling and scuba diving at Montego Bay provide unparalleled opportunities to discover the Caribbean's magnificent underwater environment. Whether you're a first-time snorkeler or a seasoned diver, Montego Bay's abundant marine life, colorful reefs, and clear waters make it a perfect site for underwater exploration and enjoyment of the beauty under the surface.

Catamaran Cruises

Catamaran tours in Montego Bay are a fun and peaceful way to take in the breathtaking coastline landscape, crystal-clear seas, and mild Caribbean wind. These cruises provide a one-of-a-kind experience by enabling you to travel around the coast, explore stunning snorkeling areas, and enjoy a range of onboard facilities. Here's a rundown of Montego Bay catamaran cruises:

Catamarans are large, sturdy, and comfortable yachts that give a smooth and fun sailing experience. As the catamaran glides across the turquoise waters of Montego Bay, you'll be able to relax on deck, soak up the sun, and enjoy the calm ocean air.

Coastal Scenery: The coastline of Montego Bay is famous for its magnificent beauty, with beautiful beaches, towering cliffs, and lush foliage. Catamaran cruises provide sweeping views of the coastline and a distinct viewpoint on Montego Bay's natural marvels.

Snorkeling Excursions: Many Montego Bay catamaran cruises offer snorkeling excursions to experience the beautiful undersea environment. You will get the opportunity to snorkel in clean, warm seas abounding with beautiful coral reefs and tropical species. Snorkeling equipment is frequently available aboard, making it easy to plunge in and enjoy the aquatic life.

Catamaran cruises often provide a variety of onboard facilities to improve your experience. You may relax on the vast sun decks, sip cool drinks from the open bar, and savor delectable meals and snacks supplied aboard. For extra amusement, some catamarans have water slides or trampolines.

Music and Entertainment: Montego Bay catamaran cruises are recognized for their vibrant and exciting environment. Local music like reggae and calypso fills the air, creating a joyous atmosphere aboard. Some cruises may include live bands or DJs on board, creating a pleasant and dynamic atmosphere throughout the voyage.

Sunset Cruises: Consider arranging a sunset catamaran sail for a romantic and unforgettable experience. It's a magnificent sight to see the sun set beyond the horizon, coloring the sky with orange and pink colours. It's a perfect place for couples or anyone looking for a peaceful and gorgeous environment.

Private cruises: Private catamaran cruises are available in Montego Bay if you want a more intimate and customized experience. You may personalize your schedule, choose your chosen activities, and enjoy the privacy of having the catamaran exclusively for yourself and your company.

The crew on catamaran cruises is noted for their warmth and friendliness. They are skilled specialists who will assure your comfort and safety during the trip. They often give information about the sites, help with snorkeling equipment, and act as hosts to create a warm and pleasurable ambiance.

Catamaran cruises are ideal for individuals, couples, families, and groups of friends. Whether you're traveling alone or with a big group, catamaran cruises provide a social atmosphere in which you may meet new people, share experiences, and make lasting memories.

Environmental Concerns: Many Montego Bay catamaran cruise providers stress sustainable and responsible tourist practices. They advocate for environmentally beneficial projects such as reef protection and reducing their carbon impact. By using these operators, you can help to preserve the natural environment of Montego Bay.

Catamaran cruises in Montego Bay combine leisure, discovery, and entertainment. Catamaran cruises provide a remarkable experience and a unique view of the gorgeous Jamaican coastline, whether you're looking for a snorkeling expedition, a romantic sunset sail, or a fun-filled group trip.

Montego Bay Golfing

Golf is a popular pastime in Montego Bay because it blends the breathtaking natural splendor of the Caribbean with world-class golf courses. Montego Bay, with its lush scenery, tropical temperature, and spectacular ocean vistas, provides an excellent golfing experience for players of all ability levels. Here's a rundown of the golf options in Montego Bay:

Championship Golf Courses: Several championship golf courses created by notable architects may be found in Montego Bay. With perfectly groomed fairways, strategically placed bunkers, and stunning water features, these courses provide players with a demanding but entertaining experience. Half Moon Golf Course, Cinnamon Hill Golf Course, and White Witch Golf Course are among the best golf courses in Montego Bay.

Spectacular landscape: Golfing in Montego Bay allows you to play among magnificent natural landscape. Many courses have spectacular vistas of the Caribbean Sea, rolling hills, and lush greenery. The contrast between the brilliant green fairways and the azure water makes a wonderfully stunning environment.

Course Designs: Montego Bay has a wide range of course designs, each with its own set of difficulties and characteristics. Golfers may test their talents in a variety of locales, ranging from coastal courses with seaside holes to courses located amid lush tropical woods.

Professional Golf Amenities: The Montego Bay golf courses provide top-notch amenities to improve your golfing experience. Clubhouses include locker rooms, pro shops, practice spaces, and food choices. Many golf courses now provide professional tuition and golf clinics for anyone wishing to improve their game.

Golf Tournaments and Events: Throughout the year, Montego Bay holds a variety of golf tournaments and events that draw players from all over the globe. These competitions allow both amateur and professional golfers to demonstrate their talents and compete in a lively and competitive environment.

Golf packages and stay-and-play options are available at many Montego Bay resorts, enabling you to combine your golfing experience with a sumptuous stay. These packages often include lodging, green fees, cart rentals, and other amenities, bringing convenience and value to dedicated golfers.

Golf schools: If you want to enhance your golfing talents or learn the game from the ground up, Montego Bay has golf schools that provide training and coaching. Experienced teachers can walk you through the basics, help you fine-tune your swing, and give you useful pointers to improve your entire game.

Golfing tournaments and Festivals: In addition to individual play, Montego Bay offers golfing tournaments and festivals that honor the sport and bring together the golfing community. These events often involve friendly tournaments, social gatherings, and networking opportunities with other golf fans.

Picturesque Drives: While driving between Montego Bay golf courses, you'll have the opportunity to enjoy picturesque drives along the coast and through the gorgeous Jamaican countryside. These drives allow extra opportunity to take in the island's natural splendor and find hidden jewels along the route.

Relaxation and leisure: Golfing in Montego Bay is more than simply a game; it's also a chance to unwind, relax, and appreciate the tranquillity of your surroundings. After a game of golf, you may recuperate and participate in leisure activities by taking use of resort facilities such as spas, pools, and restaurants.

Golf at Montego Bay has the ideal blend of difficult play, breathtaking surroundings, and opulent facilities.

Whether you're an experienced golfer or a novice, the golf courses in Montego Bay provide a great experience in a tropical paradise.

CHAPTER 8

Events and Festivals in Montego Bay

Reggae Sumfest

Reggae Sumfest is Jamaica's biggest reggae music festival and one of Montego Bay's most anticipated yearly events. It features the greatest of reggae, dancehall, and other Jamaican music genres, drawing both local and international musicians and music fans. Here's a rundown of Reggae Sumfest:

Reggae Sumfest has been hosted in Montego Bay since 1993, and its popularity has risen throughout the years. It was established to promote reggae music and celebrate Jamaica's diverse musical legacy.

The festival usually lasts several days and includes a number of pre-events, parties, and performances building up to the main event. The main stage presentations are generally conducted over two consecutive nights and include notable local and international musicians performing.

Performances: The Reggae Sumfest program includes some of the greatest stars in reggae, dancehall, and other related genres. Legends like as Bob Marley, Buju Banton, Damian Marley, Sean Paul, Shaggy, and others have performed as headliners in the past. The event also gives new artists a chance to show off their skills.

The event is held in Montego Bay's Catherine Hall Entertainment Complex. The facility has many stages, which allows for simultaneous performances and creates a dynamic environment for festival attendees.

Reggae Sumfest provides an immersive experience with live concerts, DJ sets, and sound system collisions. High-energy presentations, intriguing stage configurations, and cutting-edge sound systems will enhance the irresistible rhythms of reggae and dancehall music.

Dancehall Night: Dancehall Night, devoted to the popular dancehall music, is one of the highlights of Reggae Sumfest. This night is recognized for its high-energy performances, dancing contests, and the most recent dancehall singles. Dancehall Night attracts a lively audience and highlights the growth and effect of this genre on Jamaican music and culture.

Reggae Night at Reggae Sumfest honors the origins and spirit of reggae music. It includes soul-stirring performances by reggae veterans and modern singers, who pay respect to the genre's rich heritage while preaching themes of love, unity, and social conscience.

Street Parties: In addition to the main stage acts, Reggae Sumfest incorporates street parties and pre-events held across Montego Bay. These events provide a more personal and casual atmosphere to enjoy the captivating energy of Jamaican music and dance culture.

Cultural Experience: Reggae Sumfest is more than simply music; it also serves as a showcase for Jamaican culture. Attendees may immerse themselves in Jamaica's rich cultural tapestry, from vivid fashion and street flair to scrumptious local food.

Economic effect: The Reggae Sumfest has a substantial economic effect on Montego Bay and the Jamaican tourist sector as a whole. It draws thousands of tourists from all over the globe, boosting tourism income, creating jobs, and promoting Jamaican music and culture on a worldwide scale.

Reggae Sumfest is a celebration of Jamaica's musical legacy, as well as a chance to explore the island's addictive rhythms, vivid performances, and rich cultural tapestry. Reggae Sumfest in Montego Bay is not to be missed whether you are a reggae fan or just looking for a fantastic music festival experience.

Jamaica Food & Drink Festival

The Jamaica Food and Drink Festival is a gourmet festival hosted annually in Montego Bay and other places around Jamaica. It showcases Jamaican cuisine's distinct tastes and culinary traditions, providing a unique chance for residents and tourists to enjoy in a range of scrumptious foods and drinks. The Jamaica Food and Drink Festival is summarized below:

The Jamaica Food and Drink Festival is often a multi-day event held at different sites in Montego Bay. Each day of the festival focuses on a distinct component of Jamaican cuisine, featuring a diverse array of food and beverage options.

Culinary Delights: The event gathers some of Jamaica's best chefs, restaurants, and food artisans to display their culinary skills. Expect to enjoy a range of Jamaican foods, including classic favorites, current adaptations, and inventive fusion concoctions.

Hallmark Events: The festival includes a number of hallmark events, each with its own distinct concept and menu. Among the popular events are:

Picante: A spicy and tasty Jamaican cuisine festival, comprising meals imbued with indigenous spices and scorching tastes.

Chopstix: This event promotes the innovative use of ingredients and methods from both culinary traditions, showcasing the fusion of Jamaican and Asian cuisines.

Crisp: A seafood feast with fresh catches from Jamaica's abundant waterways served in a variety of delectable ways.

Meet Street: A colorful street food experience with food vendors, live music, and a bustling ambiance that offers a sample of Jamaica's rich street cuisine culture.

Brunch at the Gallery: A brunch event at a local gallery that blends wonderful cuisine with art and culture.

Celebrity Chefs & Cooking Demonstrations: Throughout the festival, prominent local and worldwide chefs share their knowledge via cooking demonstrations, seminars, and interactive experiences. Attendees will be able to learn new methods, acquire culinary inspiration, and get a behind-the-scenes look at the world of gastronomy.

Mixology & Beverage Tastings: The event promotes Jamaica's diverse beverage culture in addition to cuisine. Participants may sample Jamaican rum, handmade cocktails, locally produced beers, and other pleasant drinks. To promote the ingenuity and talent of

Jamaican bartenders, mixology contests and seminars are also held.

The Jamaica Food and Drink Festival extends beyond the gastronomic experience by including live music performances, cultural exhibits, and entertainment that reflect Jamaica's rich legacy and lively arts sector.

Community Engagement: By sponsoring philanthropic projects and activities, the festival hopes to give back to the local community. The event helps to improve Jamaica's culinary sector and supports the growth of local farmers, food producers, and craftsmen via collaborations with local groups.

Culinary Tourism & Promotion: The Jamaica Food and Drink Festival is important in promoting culinary tourism in Montego Bay and across Jamaica. It draws foodies, foreign tourists, and media attention by displaying Jamaica's unique culinary products and expertise.

The Jamaica Food and Drink Festival is a festival of Jamaican food, emphasizing the island's culinary heritage's tastes, inventiveness, and cultural importance. It gives chefs, culinary artisans, and beverage manufacturers a platform to demonstrate their talents and inventions while providing participants with an exceptional gourmet experience.

Celebration of Bob Marley's Birthday

The Bob Marley Birthday Celebration is an annual event conducted in Montego Bay and other regions of Jamaica to honour the iconic reggae artist Bob Marley's life and legacy. Bob Marley's birthday is commemorated with music, art, and numerous events that recognize his accomplishments as one of Jamaica's most significant individuals in music and culture. The following is a synopsis of the Bob Marley Birthday Celebration:

The Bob Marley Birthday Celebration will take held on February 6th, which is Bob Marley's birthday. The celebration is often spread out across many days, allowing for a variety of events and performances.

Music Tribute: The music of Bob Marley is central to the event. Several local and international musicians sing his renowned songs in tribute to his music, words, and message of togetherness and social justice. Live concerts and tribute acts provide a dynamic environment packed with reggae beats and good feelings.

Cultural Activities: The event will also include a variety of cultural activities that will highlight Jamaica's rich past and Rastafarian influence. Drumming sessions, traditional dances, storytelling, art displays, and artisan markets where tourists may learn about Jamaican arts and crafts may be included.

Panel Discussions and Seminars: In addition to the musical celebrations, the Bob Marley Birthday Celebration often includes panel discussions and seminars that dive into Bob Marley's life, music, and legacy. Scholars, artists, and specialists give their ideas and viewpoints on his effect on Jamaican culture and the worldwide music industry.

Tours of the Bob Marley Museum in Kingston, Jamaica: The Bob Marley Birthday Celebration is an ideal occasion to visit the Bob Marley Museum in Kingston, Jamaica. The museum, which is housed in Bob Marley's old home, provides guided tours that take tourists through his life narrative, music, and personal possessions, providing visitors with a unique insight into his life and career.

Community participation: The festival also highlights charity and community participation. Several outreach activities, humanitarian efforts, and events are arranged to help social concerns and improve impoverished areas, demonstrating Bob Marley's dedication to social change and empowerment.

Tribute Concerts and Parties: at addition to the larger concerts and shows, smaller tribute concerts and parties are often arranged at pubs, clubs, and venues across Montego Bay. These gatherings provide an open and celebratory environment, enabling participants to immerse themselves in the happy celebration of Bob Marley's music and legacy.

Food and Drinks: Jamaican cuisine plays an important part in the celebration, with food booths and merchants selling a range of traditional Jamaican meals and beverages. While taking in the celebrations, visitors may experience traditional Jamaican delicacies.

Bob Marley items: During the event, fans may buy Bob Marley items such as t-shirts, posters, music records, and souvenirs. The event often includes merchants selling a variety of branded merchandise, allowing fans to carry a piece of Bob Marley's legacy with them.

Cultural Unity and Remembrance: The Bob Marley Birthday Celebration brings together individuals from all walks of life and nations who share a passion for Bob Marley and his music. It is a time of cultural togetherness and commemoration, with fans uniting to respect his legacy and the principles he preached via his songs.

The Bob Marley Birthday Celebration in Montego Bay is a bright and uplifting event that commemorates one of Jamaica's most famous individuals via his life, music, and cultural legacy. The event highlights the essence of Bob Marley's spirit via music, art, conversations, and community participation, and continues to inspire generations of music fans worldwide.

CHAPTER 9

Useful Phrases and Vocabulary

Common Jamaican Expressions

Jamaican expressions are an integral part of the country's vibrant culture and unique dialect. They reflect the island's history, influences, and the rich linguistic blend of African, European, and Indigenous languages. Here are some common Jamaican expressions and their meanings:

"Ya mon" - This phrase is an informal way of saying "yes" or "okay." It is often used to express agreement, affirmation, or understanding.

"Mi deh yah" - Translated as "I am here," this expression is used to indicate that one is present or available.

"Likkle more" - This phrase means "see you later" or "until next time." It is a casual way of saying goodbye or farewell.

"Wah gwaan?" - A popular Jamaican greeting that translates to "What's going on?" or "What's happening?" It is often used to inquire about someone's well-being or to start a conversation.

"Mi deh pon di case" - This expression means "I am on the case" or "I am handling the situation." It implies that one is actively engaged in addressing a particular matter.

"Big up" - This phrase is used to give praise, recognition, or respect to someone. It is similar to saying "props" or "kudos."

"Bredda" or "Sistren" - These terms are used to refer to a male friend ("bredda") or a female friend ("sistren"). They signify camaraderie and closeness.

"No problem" - A widely known Jamaican expression, it means "You're welcome" or "It's okay." It reflects the laid-back and easygoing attitude often associated with Jamaican culture.

"Mi deh pan di move" - This phrase means "I am on the move" or "I am busy." It indicates that someone is actively engaged in various activities and may not be readily available.

"Mi deh pon chill" - This expression means "I am relaxing" or "I am taking it easy." It conveys a state of leisure or unwinding.

"Mi nuh know" - Translated as "I don't know," this phrase is used when one doesn't have the answer to a question or is uncertain about something.

"Mi soon come" - Similar to "I'll be right back," this expression implies that one will return shortly or complete a task in the near future.

"Yuh understand?" - Often added at the end of a sentence, this question seeks confirmation or agreement from the listener. It is equivalent to asking "Do you understand?"

"Mi belly full" - This phrase means "I am full" or "I have eaten enough." It is commonly used after enjoying a satisfying meal.

"Mi deh pon di go" - This expression signifies that someone is actively moving or traveling. It implies being on the move or in a state of constant motion.

These are just a few examples of the many colorful expressions used in Jamaican dialect. Embracing and understanding these phrases can enhance your cultural experience and help you connect with the friendly and vibrant people of Jamaica.

Basic Jamaican Patois Phrases

Jamaican Patois, also known as Jamaican Creole, is a unique language with its own grammar, vocabulary, and pronunciation. Here are some basic Jamaican Patois phrases to help you navigate conversations and immerse yourself in the local culture:

"Wha gwaan?" - Translated as "What's going on?" or "What's happening?" It is a common greeting and way to inquire about someone's well-being.

"Mi deh yah" - This phrase means "I am here" and is used to indicate your presence or availability.

"How yuh stay?" - This phrase is equivalent to asking "How are you?" or "How are you doing?"

"Mi name ____" - Use this phrase to introduce yourself by saying "My name is ____."

"Wah yuh seh?" - This expression means "What are you saying?" or "What do you say?" It is a way of asking someone for their opinion or response.

"Mi deh pon di way" - This phrase means "I am on my way" or "I am coming." It indicates that you are en route to a specific location.

"Mi cyaan manage" - Use this phrase to convey that you are unable to handle or manage a particular situation.

"Tank yuh" - This phrase is the Jamaican way of saying "Thank you."

"Mi deh pan di hustle" - This expression means "I am on the hustle" or "I am working hard." It conveys being busy or engaged in various activities.

"Wha yuh name?" - This phrase is equivalent to asking "What is your name?" It is a way to inquire about someone's identity.

"Mi deh pon di vibes" - This phrase means "I am on the vibes" or "I am feeling good." It conveys a positive and energetic state of being.

"Weh di ting deh?" - Use this expression to ask "Where is the thing?" It is a way of inquiring about the location of an object.

"One love" - This popular phrase embodies the spirit of unity, peace, and love. It is often used as a farewell or as a way of expressing goodwill.

"Mi deh pon di same page" - This expression means "I am on the same page" or "I understand." It signifies agreement or alignment with someone's thoughts or plans.

"Wha mek?" - Translated as "Why?" or "What's the reason?" It is used to inquire about the cause or reason behind something.

Remember, Jamaican Patois is a dynamic and expressive language, and the pronunciation and usage can vary across different regions and communities. Embracing these basic phrases will help you connect with the locals and immerse yourself in the rich Jamaican culture.

CHAPTER 10

Day Trip & Nearby Destination

Negril

Negril is a renowned tourist resort on Jamaica's western coast, noted for its beautiful beaches, active nightlife, and laid-back vibe. It provides the ideal combination of leisure, adventure, and natural beauty, making it a must-see destination for visitors. Here is a rundown of everything Negril has to offer:

Negril is notable for its pristine Seven Mile Beach, which is widely recognized as one of the most beautiful beaches in the Caribbean. Its crystal-clear blue seas, smooth white sand, and palm-fringed coastline make it ideal for sunbathing, swimming, and participating in different water sports.

Cliff Jumping at Rick's Café: Rick's Café is well-known in Negril for its cliff diving and stunning sunset views. Adrenaline junkies may jump over the cliffs into the Caribbean Sea, while others can unwind with live music, delectable cuisine, and beverages.

Negril Lighthouse: A historic landmark, the Negril Lighthouse gives panoramic views of the coastline. Climb to the top of the lighthouse for spectacular views of the Caribbean Sea and neighboring locations.

Water Sports and Activities: Negril has a variety of water sports and activities to suit adventure seekers. There are several activities available to explore the colorful marine life and enjoy the warm Caribbean seas, ranging from snorkeling and scuba diving to kayaking, paddleboarding, and jet skiing.

Negril is famous for its stunning West End Cliffs, in addition to its gorgeous beaches. These craggy limestone cliffs provide spectacular vistas and are ideal for cliff diving, snorkeling, and discovering secret caves and coves.

Negril Craft Market: The Negril Craft Market is a must-see for anybody interested in shopping and local crafts. Local craftsmen sell a wide range of handcrafted things, including artwork, jewelry, apparel, and souvenirs.

Music and Live Entertainment: Negril is a thriving center for reggae music and live entertainment. Many pubs and clubs include live bands, DJs, and local entertainers, which creates a dynamic scene for music fans to dance the night away.

Coral Reefs and Marine Parks: Negril has some of Jamaica's top coral reefs and marine parks. Visitors may go snorkeling or diving to discover the underwater environment, which is alive with colorful fish, coral formations, and other marine life.

Restaurants & small food: There are several eating alternatives in Negril, ranging from small eateries providing traditional Jamaican food to sophisticated restaurants serving worldwide specialties. Don't pass up the chance to sample jerk chicken, fresh fish, and other classic Jamaican cuisine.

Relaxation and Wellness: Negril is an excellent place to unwind and rejuvenate. Many resorts and spas provide wellness retreats, yoga courses, and spa treatments to help you relax and discover inner peace in the middle of tranquil settings.

Negril's relaxed atmosphere, magnificent natural beauty, and diverse range of activities make it a location that appeals to a wide range of interests and tastes. Negril offers something for everyone, whether you're looking for adventure, leisure, or a vibrant nightlife scene.

Ocho Rios

Ocho Rios is a dynamic and busy town on Jamaica's northern coast. It is a well-known tourist destination due to its stunning beaches, lush tropical surroundings, and fascinating attractions. Here is a summary of everything Ocho Rios has to offer:

Dunn's River Falls: The renowned Dunn's River Falls is one of Ocho Rios' principal attractions. This breathtaking natural marvel is a flowing waterfall that tourists may climb with the assistance of professional guides. The ascent is both invigorating and exciting, with chances to bathe in natural lakes along the route.

Mystic Mountain: Mystic Mountain is a must-see sight in Ocho Rios for adventure lovers. It has a variety of exhilarating activities, such as a sky explorer chairlift, jungle bobsled rides, and zip-lining excursions. The attraction also offers spectacular views of the surrounding area.

Dolphin Cove is a marine park in Ocho Rios where tourists may interact with dolphins, swim with sharks and stingrays, and participate in other aquatic activities. It's an excellent spot for families and animal enthusiasts to learn about and enjoy Jamaica's marine life.

Fern Gully: Nature enthusiasts will like Fern Gully, a picturesque meandering road that goes through a thick jungle. The route is bordered by several fern species, providing a one-of-a-kind and lovely ambience. Visitors may drive through this natural beauty or enjoy a guided tour.

Blue Hole: Also known as the Secret Falls, the Blue Hole is a hidden treasure in Ocho Rios. It has a lovely environment, with turquoise pools and flowing waterfalls. Visitors may swim, dive, or leap into the cool water, or just rest and take in the scenery.

James Bond Beach: As the name implies, James Bond Beach is a popular destination for lovers of the legendary film series. It has a lovely sandy beach, clean seas for swimming, and water sports. The Oracabessa Bay Fish Sanctuary is also located on the shore, making it an ideal location for snorkeling and discovering marine life.

The White River is a beautiful river that runs through Ocho Rios. Visitors may enjoy the quiet environment and beautiful surroundings by tubing or rafting down the river. It's a terrific opportunity to take in Jamaica's natural beauty while drifting along the moderate currents.

Shaw Park Gardens: Shaw Park Gardens is a botanical park on the outskirts of Ocho Rios. It has a diverse collection of tropical plants, flowers, and trees, as well as breathtaking views of the town and shoreline. Visitors may enjoy a leisurely walk around the grounds while admiring the vibrant flora.

Turtle River Falls and Gardens: Another lovely botanical garden in Ocho Rios is Turtle River Falls and Gardens. It has magnificent landscapes, waterfalls, and natural ponds. Visitors may stroll around the garden's walks, bathe in the pools, or just rest in the tranquil setting.

Shopping and Dining: There are various artisan markets, souvenir stores, and shopping complexes in Ocho Rios. The town is also well-known for its lively nightlife, with a wide range of restaurants, pubs, and clubs serving local food, live music, and entertainment.

Ocho Rios is a vacation location that combines natural beauty, adventure, and cultural activities. Ocho Rios provides something for everyone, whether you're looking for outdoor sports, leisure, or an investigation of Jamaican culture.

Falmouth

Falmouth is a historic town on Jamaica's northern coast. It has a rich history, well-preserved Georgian buildings, and a picturesque shoreline. Falmouth is a one-of-a-kind combination of culture, legacy, and natural beauty. Here is a summary of what Falmouth has to offer:

Falmouth is home to the historic Falmouth Cruise Port, which serves as a port of call for numerous cruise ships. The port area is stunningly planned, with stores, restaurants, and entertainment choices galore. Visitors may walk about the neighborhood, buy souvenirs, and enjoy the bustling environment.

Georgian Architecture: Falmouth has one of the Caribbean's outstanding collections of Georgian architecture. The historic core of the town is a joy to explore, with well-preserved buildings displaying exquisite features and brilliant colors. Take a stroll around the streets of Falmouth to appreciate the architecture and learn about the town's historical history.

Hampden Estate: A visit to Hampden Estate is a must for rum fans. This historic rum distillery has been producing rum for over 260 years and provides guided tours during which visitors may learn about the rum-making process and taste several rum kinds. For those interested in the island's rum legacy, it's a fascinating experience.

Martha Brae River Rafting: Located just outside of Falmouth, the Martha Brae River provides a peaceful and gorgeous experience. Visitors may board a bamboo raft escorted by an experienced raft captain and float along the river while surrounded by lush foliage and attractive scenery.

Greenwood Great home: The Greenwood Great House is a historic plantation home in Falmouth. It was the Barrett family's residence before becoming a museum displaying the family's collection of antique furniture, paintings, and antiquities. Visitors to the mansion may tour it and learn about Jamaica's colonial past.

Burwood Beach is a lovely length of coastline near Falmouth with smooth sand and gorgeous blue waves. It's an excellent location for sunbathing, swimming, and picnics. The beach is often less crowded than other prominent Jamaican beaches, resulting in a more calm and tranquil ambiance.

Glistening Waters: Glistening Waters is a natural phenomena known as the Luminous Lagoon, and it is located in neighboring Falmouth. Microorganisms inhabit this bioluminescent bay, which emits a blue light when disturbed, producing a wonderful and otherworldly experience. Visitors may see the dazzling waters by taking a boat excursion at night.

Food & Dining: Falmouth has a wide range of dining choices, from traditional Jamaican fare to foreign fare. Traditional Jamaican cuisine such as jerk chicken, curry goat, ackee and saltfish, as well as fresh seafood and other dishes, are available.

The Albert George Shopping and Historical Centre in Falmouth blends retail therapy with historical exhibitions. Visitors may buy for apparel, souvenirs, and local crafts while learning about Falmouth's history and culture via interactive exhibitions and displays.

The Outameni Experience is a cultural site in Falmouth that provides tourists with an insight into Jamaican history, music, dance, and tradition. Visitors may immerse themselves in Jamaica's diverse culture and customs via interactive displays, live performances, and storytelling.

Falmouth offers guests a one-of-a-kind and immersive experience, combining history, culture, and natural beauty. Whether you're interested in colonial architecture, learning about the island's rum past, or just relaxing along the shore, Falmouth offers something for everyone.

Kingston

Kingston, Jamaica's capital city, is a dynamic and busy metropolis on the island's southern coast. It is not only Jamaica's biggest city, but also the country's cultural, economic, and political hub. Here is a summary of everything Kingston has to offer:

The Bob Marley Museum, housed in the old home of reggae icon Bob Marley, is one of Kingston's must-see sites. The museum provides an intriguing look into Bob Marley's life and career, showing his personal artifacts, souvenirs, and recording studio.

Devon House: Devon House is a magnificently renovated home that provides an insight into Jamaica's colonial history. Visitors may enjoy the large halls and beautiful grounds, as well as the famed Devon House ice cream, which is recognized for its wonderful varieties.

National Gallery of Jamaica: Art lovers will enjoy a visit to the National Gallery of Jamaica, which holds a large collection of Jamaican artwork, such as paintings, sculptures, and mixed media projects. The gallery exhibits both current and historical artifacts, giving visitors a glimpse into Jamaican art and culture.

Emancipation Park: Located in the center of Kingston, Emancipation Park is a calm haven. It has nicely designed gardens, jogging pathways, and a monument commemorating slavery's abolition in Jamaica. The park is a great place to unwind, exercise, and picnic.

Port Royal: A visit to Port Royal is a must for history aficionados. Port Royal, formerly an infamous pirate refuge, is now a historical monument with vestiges of its rich nautical heritage. Visitors may learn about the city's pirate history by visiting the Giddy House, Fort Charles, and the Port Royal Museum.

Kingston Harbour: Kingston Harbour is one of the world's biggest natural harbors and provides scenic views of the city's skyline. Visitors may explore the port by boat, go to Lime Cay for a day of sunbathing and swimming, or just enjoy the riverside environment.

The Hope Botanical Gardens and Zoo is a huge green park in Kingston that features a broad range of tropical plants, flowers, and trees. The zoo is home to a variety of animal species, including birds, reptiles, and mammals, making it a popular family destination.

Coronation Market: Coronation Market is Kingston's biggest and busiest market, with a lively atmosphere and a diverse selection of fresh vegetables, local handicrafts, and traditional Jamaican cuisine. Visitors may immerse themselves in the bright spirit of the market and get firsthand knowledge of the local culture.

Kingston's nightlife culture is bustling, with various pubs, clubs, and live music venues. From reggae and dancehall to jazz and calypso, music fans may enjoy the beat and moods of Jamaican music in a variety of styles.

Jamaican National Heroes Park is an important historical landmark in Kingston that serves as the last resting place for many of Jamaica's national heroes and noteworthy personalities. The park is attractively designed, with monuments and sculptures celebrating Jamaica's history and traditions.

Kingston has a distinct mix of history, culture, and urban life. Kingston offers a multitude of activities and experiences to offer, whether you want to explore the reggae music scene, learn about Jamaican history, or immerse yourself in the local culture.

CHAPTER 11

Shopping in Montego Bay

Craft Fairs

Montego Bay's craft markets are dynamic centres where tourists can immerse themselves in local culture, discover one-of-a-kind handcrafted products, and engage with brilliant Jamaican craftsmen. These markets sell a broad range of products, including as traditional artwork, jewelry, apparel, wood carvings, and other items. Here's a rundown of Montego Bay's artisan markets:

Harbour Street Craft Market: Harbour Street Craft Market, located near the Montego Bay Cruise Ship Terminal, is a popular location for travelers searching for traditional Jamaican crafts. This market is recognized for its vibrant atmosphere and wide variety of handcrafted handicrafts. Visitors may peruse kiosks displaying bright paintings, woven baskets, beaded jewelry, and other traditional goods.

The Old Fort Craft Market, located inside the ancient walls of an old fort, offers a one-of-a-kind shopping experience. It showcases a variety of local craftspeople displaying their work. Hand-carved wooden sculptures, straw hats, batik garments, and other beautifully created products are available to visitors. The market's position also provides beautiful views of the bay.

Crafts Market Village: Crafts Market Village is a lively market with various merchants located in Montego Bay's famed Hip Strip district. It sells Jamaican crafts such as hand-painted artwork, leather products, pottery, and Rastafarian-inspired things. The market is an excellent spot to discover one-of-a-kind items and souvenirs.

Montego Craft Market: This market, located near the Montego Bay Marine Park, highlights the abilities of local artists. It sells a variety of goods, such as handcrafted jewelry, wood sculptures, tie-dye apparel, and woven items. To receive the greatest pricing, visitors may participate in friendly bargaining with the merchants.

Gloucester Avenue artisan Market: This artisan market is located along Gloucester Avenue, popularly known as the Hip Strip, and is conveniently accessible for people touring the neighborhood. It sells Jamaican items such as traditional paintings, batik textiles, beading, and straw crafts. The market offers a vibrant atmosphere as well, with street performers and local musicians providing entertainment.

Quality and Authenticity: Montego Bay craft fairs are noted for selling genuine Jamaican items manufactured by local artists. These crafts represent the island's rich cultural past and are often made utilizing traditional methods and materials. Visitors may be certain that the things they buy are authentic and help the local economy.

Cultural Experience: Visiting Montego Bay artisan markets allows you to interact with Jamaican culture firsthand. Interacting with the craftsmen, learning about their creative skills, and hearing the tales behind their works enriches the purchasing experience with depth and purpose. It's an opportunity to admire creative traditions handed down through centuries.

Bargaining: In Jamaican artisan markets, bargaining is widespread. Visitors may bargain with merchants to obtain a fair deal. Bargaining should be approached with respect and a polite attitude, since it is part of the local culture. Remember that the ultimate price agreed upon should satisfy both parties.

Supporting Local Artists: Visiting Montego Bay craft fairs enables tourists to directly support local craftsmen and their livelihoods. By buying handcrafted items, you help to ensure the survival of Jamaica's traditional arts and crafts. It's an important approach to understand and maintain local culture.

Craft markets provide a variety of unique products that encapsulate the character of Montego Bay and Jamaica. Hand-painted artwork showing Jamaican landscapes, handmade jewelry, or a wooden sculpture highlighting local fauna are all treasured keepsakes of your time to Montego Bay.

Montego Bay's craft markets provide a genuine and fascinating shopping experience. They are not just locations to purchase souvenirs, but also places to engage with local craftsmen, immerse yourself in Jamaican culture, and bring home one-of-a-kind items that represent the island's colorful personality.

Duty-Free Shopping

Duty-free shopping in Montego Bay is a popular pastime for travelers wishing to save money on a range of items. Duty-free shopping opportunities in Montego Bay include establishments situated at the airport, downtown neighborhoods, and major resorts. Here's a rundown of Montego Bay's duty-free shopping:

Sangster International Airport: The Sangster International Airport in Montego Bay includes a number of duty-free stores where tourists may stock up on items before their flight. These stores sell a broad range of products, including luxury items, jewelry, watches, apparel, electronics, and local souvenirs. Duty-free stores at airports are a useful choice for last-minute shopping or picking up things upon arrival.

The Shoppes at Rose Hall: Located in Montego Bay's Rose Hall neighborhood, The Shoppes at Rose Hall is a popular shopping destination with a variety of duty-free businesses. Luxury brands, designer apparel, accessories, cosmetics, and other items are available to visitors. The complex also features restaurants, cafés, and entertainment choices, making it a popular shopping and leisure destination.

Freeport retail Village: Freeport Shopping Village is a retail center in Montego Bay located near the cruise ship terminal. It provides duty-free shopping with an emphasis on jewelry, watches, diamonds, and gemstones. Visitors may browse a range of businesses that sell high-quality jewelry at tax-free costs. For a well-rounded shopping experience, the town also offers eating and live entertainment.

Hotel shops and Resorts: Many Montego Bay hotels and resorts offer their own duty-free shops, which enable visitors to shop for a variety of things without leaving the site. Clothing, accessories, local crafts, and souvenirs are among the items available at these businesses. Guests may enjoy the convenience of shopping inside the hotel while benefiting from duty-free rates.

Tips for Duty-Free Shopping:

Here are a few pointers to help you get the most out of your duty-free shopping experience in Montego Bay:

Check the Allowances: Before making your purchases, get acquainted with your own country's duty-free allowances. This will assist you in staying inside the limits and avoiding any customs hassles upon your return.

Compare rates: While duty-free shopping provides tax-free rates, it's still a good idea to browse around to obtain the best value. To make educated purchase selections, compare costs online or in local businesses.

Maintain Receipts and documents: It is critical to maintain your duty-free receipts and any essential documents. This is necessary for customs and may be required for warranty or refund reasons.

Be Aware of limits: When it comes to duty-free shopping, some things may have limits or limitations. Alcohol, cigarettes, and luxury products may be subject to additional rules, so be aware of any limits before making your purchases.

Stick to reputed Duty-Free stores and Retailers: To assure the authenticity and quality of the items you buy, shop at reputed duty-free stores and retailers. Look for well-known brands or businesses that have been recommended by reputable sources.

Duty-free shopping in Montego Bay provides guests with a simple and tax-free shopping experience. You'll discover a broad choice of products to meet your interests and budget, whether you're seeking for luxury things, jewelry, apparel, or local souvenirs. Remember to be aware of any limits, compare costs, and retain all relevant papers for a pleasant and pleasurable purchasing experience.

Souvenirs and Local Products

When visiting Montego Bay, you'll discover a diverse selection of souvenirs and locally produced goods that encapsulate the spirit of Jamaican culture. These one-of-a-kind things enable you to take a bit of Montego Bay home with you and serve as recollections of your amazing stay. Consider the following popular souvenirs and local products:

Jamaican Rum: Jamaica is famed for its rum, and many tourists like taking back a bottle of true Jamaican rum. Look for well-known brands like as Appleton Estate or Hampden Estate, which are recognized for producing high-quality rums. Flavored rums blended with local fruits and spices are also available, providing a one-of-a-kind taste experience.

Jamaican Coffee: Jamaica produces some of the world's best coffee. Blue Mountain Coffee, cultivated in Jamaica's Blue Mountains, is prized for its smooth taste and fragrant character. To get a taste of Jamaica at home, look for certified Blue Mountain Coffee beans or ground coffee.

Jamaican Spices & Seasonings: Jamaican cuisine is famed for its robust and savory meals, and you can bring the flavor of Jamaica home with you by buying local spices and seasonings. Jerk seasoning, a famous spice combination used in Jamaican cookery, as well as additional spices such as allspice, scotch bonnet peppers, and curry powder, should be sought for.

Jamaican Artwork: Montego Bay is home to many excellent artists, and there is a wide range of artwork available that depicts Jamaican culture and scenery. Look for paintings, sculptures, and handmade objects that represent the island's rich colors and energy. Local art galleries and craft fairs are excellent locations to locate one-of-a-kind items.

Jamaican goods & Souvenirs: The artisan markets in Montego Bay are treasure troves of handcrafted goods and souvenirs. Items to look out for include woven baskets, straw hats, wood sculptures, beaded jewelry, and tie-dye apparel. Not only are these crafts attractive, but they also showcase Jamaican traditions and workmanship.

Reggae Music and Bob Marley Memorabilia: Reggae music originated in Jamaica, and you can discover a wide range of reggae records, CDs, and memorabilia at Montego Bay. Bob Marley stuff, such as T-shirts, posters, and audio compilations, is readily available and enables you to honor this legendary musician's legacy.

Jamaican Bath and Body Products: Pamper yourself with Jamaican bath and body products produced with natural ingredients and tropical smells. Soaps, lotions, oils, and bath salts packed with substances like coconut, aloe vera, and Jamaican plant extracts are ideal. These items are wonderful presents or a nice memento of your trip to Montego Bay.

Jamaican clothes and Accessories: Montego Bay has a wide selection of Jamaican clothes and accessories. Look for colourful patterns and designs inspired by Jamaican culture in clothes such as dresses, blouses, and swimwear. Handmade items such as beaded jewelry, straw hats, and woven purses are also available.

Jamaican Books & Literature: If you want to learn more about Jamaican history, culture, or literature, try buying books written by Jamaicans. Look for works by well-known writers including Louise Bennett-Coverley,

Claude McKay, and Marlon James. You may also discover books about Jamaican mythology, food, and travel guides to help you learn more about the island.

Local cuisine and Condiments: Don't forget to carry some Jamaican delicacies home with you by buying local cuisine and condiments. Look for Jamaican jerk sauce, spicy pepper sauce, tropical fruit jams and preserves, and so on. These goods enable you to reproduce Jamaican cuisine or add a Jamaican flavour to your home-cooked meals.

It's crucial to support local companies and craftsmen while shopping for souvenirs and local items in Montego Bay. To locate real and one-of-a-kind things, go to artisan fairs, art galleries, and specialized stores. Remember to bargain at marketplaces, but also recognize the worth of handcrafted artistry. Buying souvenirs and local items not only enables you to take a piece of Montego Bay home with you, but it also helps the local economy and maintains the island's lively culture.

CONCLUSION

Finally, Montego Bay is a bustling and diversified destination with something for everyone. Montego Bay has a lot to offer tourists, from its beautiful beaches and crystal-clear seas to its rich history and cultural attractions. Whether you're looking for relaxation and leisure, adventure and outdoor activities, or immersion in Jamaican culture, Montego Bay has a variety of experiences to suit your needs.

The warm welcome and pleasant grins of the natives will capture you from the minute you arrive in Montego Bay. The dynamic and energetic mood is created by the city's bustling atmosphere, colorful marketplaces, and throbbing reggae music. You may eat wonderful Jamaican food, drink world-class rum, and learn about the city's cultural history at museums, historic sites, and festivals.

Montego Bay does not disappoint when it comes to natural beauty. Sunbathing, swimming, and water sports are available on the beautiful beaches of Doctor's Cave Beach and Cornwall Beach. The verdant mountains and rivers that surround the city are ideal for hiking, ziplining, and river rafting experiences. You may also experience the underwater world by going on snorkeling and scuba diving tours to see beautiful coral reefs and marine life.

Montego Bay accommodations serve to a wide range of budgets and interests, ranging from luxury resorts and all-inclusive hotels to lovely guesthouses and vacation rentals. There are several options to rest and revitalize, including spa treatments, yoga lessons, and seaside sunbathing.

Beyond Montego Bay, surrounding attractions include Dunn's River Falls in Ocho Rios, Negril's famed Seven Mile Beach, and Falmouth's historic ruins. Each site has its own distinct experiences and features, adding to your Jamaican vacation.

To guarantee a comfortable and memorable stay, educate yourself with local traditions and etiquette, as well as health and safety concerns. Understanding visa requirements and organizing your trip properly can also help to ensure a pleasant travel experience.

With its gorgeous scenery, rich culture, and friendly people, Montego Bay really represents the spirit of Jamaica. Montego Bay welcomes you with open arms, eager to create wonderful moments that will last a lifetime, whether you're a beach lover, an adventure seeker, a history buff, or a gourmet. So pack your luggage, embrace the Jamaican culture, and prepare for an unforgettable adventure in Montego Bay.

Printed in Great Britain
by Amazon